FOREWORD

THE intention underlying this book is to give genetic account of what Marx and the Marxists call "Utopian Socialism", with particular reference to its postulate of a renewal of society through a renewal of its cell-tissue. I am not concerned to survey the development of an idea, but to sketch the picture of an idea in process of development. The fundamental question in the making of such a picture is—as in the making of all pictures—the question of what one has to leave out. Only so much of the massive material seemed to me to be relevant as was essential to a consideration of the idea itself. It is not the false turnings that are important for us, but the single broad highway into which they invariably lead. From the historical process the idea itself rises up before eyes.

There was yet another, if narrower, vista that had to be opened: the one shewing the bold but precarious attempts to bring the idea into reality. Only after that had been done was the ground cleared for a critical exposition of the theoretical and practical relation of Marxism to the idea of structural renewal—a relation which could only be hinted at in an introductory manner at the beginning of the book. At the end, in a kind of epilogue, I had to speak of one particular attempt, the immediate knowledge of which was the occasion for writing this book. I have naturally not described or reported it in detail, only thrown light on its inner connexion with the idea—as an attempt that did not fail.

The chapter preceding the epilogue sums up my own attitude to the idea, which could otherwise only be read between the lines; moreover it was necessary to point out its significance in the present hour of decision.

The book was completed in the spring of 1945; the Hebrew edition appeared in the following year.

MARTIN BUBER.

Jerusalem 1949.

Martin Buber was born in Vienna and studied at the Universities of Vienna, Leipzig, Berlin and Munich. He was professor of religion and ethics at the University of Frankfurt from 1924 to 1933. From 1938 until his retirement in 1951 he was professor of social philosophy at the Hebrew University in Jerusalem.

One of the most outstanding religious philosophers of our time, Dr. Buber has been active in the Zionist movement and the revival of Hasidic thought. His works include a German translation of the Bible, *For the Sake of Heaven, Good and Evil, I and Thou, Israel and the World, Between Man and Man,* which has already been published as a Beacon Paperback, and numerous other books and articles in the fields of Biblical scholarship, religious existentialism, and comparative religion.

MARTIN BUBER

PATHS
IN UTOPIA

Translated by
R. F. C. HULL

Introduction by EPHRAIM FISCHOFF

BEACON PRESS, BOSTON

ACKNOWLEDGMENT

THE translator would like to express his most cordial thanks to the author for his great help in the preparation of this volume, both as regards the translation and the correction of proofs. He is also indebted to Mr. Paul Derrick for checking the titles of certain books herein mentioned.

INTRODUCTION

The eightieth birthday of Martin Buber on February 8, 1958, and his concomitant visit in this country for a series of lectures, have stimulated a series of publications on or about Buber and a reissue of some of his works. With this edition of his *Paths in Utopia*, the Beacon Press joins in the expression of homage to one of the universal men of our time, who is at once scholar and educator, seer and prophet.

Many are the sources of Martin Buber's fame, and the manifestations of his universality. The significant impact of his personality upon our generation is due to his many-faceted cultural achievements. These are both Judaistic and general, comprising both theoretical and applied studies in various humanistic and sociological areas as well as in religion. He is not only one of the foremost living philosophers of Judaism, possibly its most persuasive exponent in the world's parliament of religions, and a unique interpreter of Jewish folklore as developed in the Hasidic evangelical movement, but he is also a remarkable translator of the Bible into an incomparable poetic version. He is a distinctive social philosopher, and a significant exponent of religious socialism in the great tradition of utopian social thought.

Throughout his religious and metaphysical labors the sociological interest — of which this study in utopian socialism is only one aspect — looms large; and consequently his social philosophy is religious at its core. Influenced by the pioneer work of modern German sociology, Ferdinand Toennies' *Community and Society (Gemeinschaft und Gesellschaft,* 1887), Buber became one of the professorial socialists of the German tradition; and from other thought currents of the *fin de siècle* in his own country and in general European thought, Buber imbibed a deep concern

with the restoration of true community. But Buber's professorial socialism differed from that of the other *Kathed-
ersozialisten*, even from that of the aforementioned Toennies, in that he was consistently a doughty protagonist of
social meliorism only if it retained a strongly religious
basis; i.e., only if it quested for a regenerated man in a restructured society.

Buber's espousal of utopian socialism was the result
of several interacting factors, some distinctively Jewish and
some reflecting distinctive aspects of twentieth-century Oc-
cidental culture, particularly in Germany. The former comprised his interpretation of prophetic Judaism as achieved
and manifested anew in the Jewish evangelical movement
known as Hasidism; and his particular understanding of
and activities on behalf of Zionism, construed as a movement of ethnic or national regeneration. Some of the factors
deriving from the general culture included his study of
Toennies' *Community and Society*, with its profound criticisms of developed capitalist society, which influenced all
of German sociology. There were also various currents of
thought and organizations among German intellectuals, pro-
fessors and clergy, designed to combat the inequities of
capitalism and to recreate a true community — a trend and
yearning reflected in the literature and youth movement of
the day.

Professor Buber became intimately acquainted with one
type of cooperative living — that of the *Kvutza* — the
communitarian colony of the Jewish colonists in Israel.
As a refugee from Nazi Germany in 1938, he settled in Israel
where he became professor of social philosophy at the
Hebrew University in Jerusalem, and had occasion to
study the *Kvutza,* its ideology, and its place in the whole
stream of utopian thinking. His analysis of the history of
utopian thought and his observations on the operation of
the *Kvutza* strengthened his belief that this particular
manifestation of utopian socialist thought had not failed
as a great historical experiment in restructuring society,
although admittedly much remained to be accomplished

before the experiment could be accounted a success, and many perils and impediments lurked in the time ahead. Nevertheless, Buber's knowledge of this "experiment that did not fail" was what stimulated him to write *Paths in Utopia.*

Buber's researches into the lore and history of Hasidism had provided him with an ideal type of a truly humane community, and his immersion in Biblical doctrine had given him unusual preparation for understanding the nature of messianism, as a permanent quest of man for a better world order based on spiritual perspectives. It will be recalled that Buber started as an interpreter of the foundations of Hasidism, the seminal ideas of which — and in a larger sense of all authentic Judaism — he considered to be unity, conduct, and the future. His whole subsequent evolution as a religious existentialist philosopher, his system of "dialogical life," his interpretation of social issues and his contributions to education, psychotherapy, and social philosophy, all flowed out of this primary orientation to the cardinal spiritual tenets of central prophetic Judaism as he interpreted it.

In the two years before World War I Buber had devoted himself to the consideration of various theoretical and practical problems — at the center of which stood the problem of regenerating man's spirit and redirecting human history — which he construed as being fundamentally a problem of education. A major factor in Buber's preoccupation with social thought was his continuing concern with Zionism which antedated the turn of the century.

Increasingly concerned with the deeper significance of Zionism as a creative philosophy for the modern Jew, which might accomplish the fortification of group loyalty as well as the deepening and intensification of humanity, Buber saw ever more clearly the need of educational effort. If the profound values of community were to be transmitted, they would first have to be reawakened in the new generation.

In 1913 Buber together with Erich Kahler and Arthur Salz summoned a conference in Berlin designed to plan the establishment of a Jewish college in Germany, to inaugurate the education of the coming generation in the sense of a true and vital Judaism, which hopefully would exert an influence beyond Jewish circles in advancing a general cultural and religious renewal. In this quest Buber was in rapport with basic trends of the time, for as Ernst Troeltsch remarked in *Der Historismus und seine Ueberwindung:* "On all sides there was a demand for more rootedness and community." In 1914 Buber met in Potsdam with such figures as Gustav Landauer, Florence Christian Rang, Theodor Daeubler and other significant figures in European life to form a strong cultural influence in behalf of international unity. Romain Rolland and Walter Rathenau were also interested in the progress of the group. But the outbreak of World War I put the quietus to this effort.

Buber was an earnest student of basic works in modern social thought by such thinkers as Wilhelm Dilthey, Georg Simmel and Max Weber. He projected and edited an interesting series of forty popular monographs on sociological and psychological topics, under the general title "Society" *(Die Gesellschaft)*, opening with a work on the proletariat by Werner Sombart and including a piece on religion by Georg Simmel and one on revolution by Gustav Landauer. The latter, a notable German socialist and man of letters, who occupied an important position in the first socialist government of German, exerted a profound influence on Buber's religious socialism and after the assassination of his beloved friend, Buber wrote a memorial essay about him and issued some of his unpublished works.

Essentially, the present volume is concerned with the repristination of the word "utopia," which, in the interpretation of Buber has been victimized in the course of the political struggle of Marxism against other forms of socialism and movements of social reform. In his struggle to achieve dominance for his idiosyncratic system of socialism, Marx employed "utopia" as the ultimate term of pejoration to damn all "prehistoric" (i.e. pre-Marxian) social systems as unscientific and futilitarian, in contrast to the allegedly scientific and inevitable character of his system of historical materialism. As Marxian socialism scored its massive victories, utopian socialism or utopianism appeared thoroughly discredited and doomed to the museum of intellectual aberrations. The signal victory of the proletariat in the titanic revolutionary struggle in Russia, culminating in the domination of the Bolsheviks, would, it was felt, demonstrate finally the utter validity of Marxian socialism. But the numerous failures of the Soviet Union to achieve true socialism in the decades that have passed and the diverse poignant frustrations and disillusionments with the "God that failed" have re-awakened an interest in utopian socialism, and have led not a few to feel, as Buber expresses it, that utopian and not Marxist socialism "may well be clearing the way for the structure of the coming society." Recent years have seen a spate of books concerned with a reconsideration of utopian thought, from Lewis Mumford's *The Story of Utopias* (1922) and J. O. Hertzler's *History of Utopian Thought* (1926) to Karl Mannheim's *Ideology and Utopia* (trans., 1936), Harry Ross' *Utopias Old and New* (1938), Marie Louise Berneri's *Journey Through Utopia* (1950), Raymond Ruyer's *L'Utopie et les Utopies* (1950), Glenn Negley and J. Max Patrick's *The Quest for Utopia* (1952), and Henrik F. Infield's *Utopia and Experiment — Essays in the Sociology of Cooperation* (1958). Yet another expression of the same interest is David Riesman's essay on community planning and industrial society ("Some Observations on Community Plans and Utopia," *Yale Law Journal,* December 1947, pp. 173ff.), which starts with a declaration that "a revival of the tradition of Utopian thinking seems to me one of the important intellectual tasks of today." Riesman's analysis is based on a study of community in modern technological society from the perspective of a progressive architect willing to envisage "utopian" changes in the quest for a genuine community life which would overcome the fateful separation of production from consumption that is construed as the primary cause of alienation in the life of modern man. (Percival and Paul Goodman, *Communitas: Means of Liveli-hood and Ways of Life*, 1947) . In addition there have been numerous studies of various contemporary experiments in cooperative or communitarian living such as the studies of the *Kibbutz* in Israel by Henrik Infield.

This volume purports to provide a re-examination of the utopian ideal — and the permanent value of this aspiration in the life of mankind. In its endeavor to rescue a word from oblivion and to restore it to proper esteem in the mind of mankind, the work provides an essay in semantics. Buber has the conviction that socialism has become lost in a blind alley from which it can be rescued partly by a re-evaluation of the true significance of the maligned term "utopian." But what sets this work apart from other his-tories of the utopian thought or quest is Buber's total religious philosophy. Here is a social theorist living in the post-Stalin and post-Hitler era who, despite his experi-ences of the horrors of World War II, retains his faith in man's need and capacity for regeneration and his inalien-able quest for a synthesis of religion and socialism. Buber provides a survey of the development of utopian thought, covering such figures as Fourier, Saint-Simon, Owen and Proudhon. From these Buber proceeds to an evaluation of the achievement of Marx, stressing the continuing utopian element in the latter's thought, despite his derisive rejection of utopianism.

Buber demonstrates the relationships of Marx and Engels to those early formulators of the socialist ideal of the uni-versal transformation of society. By virtue of the criticism by Marx and Engels the term "utopian" came to denote social thinkers who had not taken account of modern in-dustrial development, the class struggle and the unique function of the proletariat therein. Thereafter utopian socialism became the "dirty word" of social thought and a synonym for delusion, obscurantism, or ideological obfusca-tion — a completely negligible factor in the period of modern economic evolution. This arrogant dismissal of Utopian thinkers, both "prehistoric" and post-Marxian, was effected despite the admission by Engels that German socialist theory would never forget the illustrious labors of the pre-Marxist romantic social philosophers.

An examination of the thought of Lenin follows, culminating in an analysis of the failure of the socialist ideal in communism. This is followed by one of the most interesting chapters, "An Experiment That Did Not Fail," in which Buber analyzes the communitarian movement of the Zionist *Kibbutz*, of which he was one of the ideological godfathers, and argues that this venture in socialism did *not* founder precisely because it has remained dedicated to the ideal of the emergence of a new community.

Buber also carried into his understanding of sociology the same perspectives he applied to Marxism. He interpreted sociology (founded, in his judgment, by Saint-Simon) as a critical science, designed to overcome the crises of the age; and he saw both Auguste Comte and Lorenz von Stein as dedicated to the conquest of the inner contradictions of the age through adequate knowledge of social conditions.

Even after Comte had departed from the doctrine of his teacher, Saint-Simon, he still characterized Saint-Simon's social program with a formula that accurately described his own intellectual project: *une régéneration sociale fondée sur une rénovation mentale.* He emphasized that all schemes for social reorganization based on the profound moral and political anarchy of the time required a prior spiritual reorganization of society, the creation of a new spiritual attitude to prevent the deterioration and corruption of institutions. In one of Buber's essays, "The Demand of the Spirit and Historical Reality," he adverts to the insights of Siegfried Landshut, who interprets modern sociology, in his *Kritik der Soziologie,* as an expression of the criticism or critique of historico-social reality. But while Buber admits the partial truth of the need for this assertion, he stresses the necessity of continuing to work for the transformation of the spirit, without which any alteration of institutions is doomed to failure. It is inevitable that man must transform himself to the same degree that he changes his institutions, lest, as Buber puts it, the new house man hopes to erect become his burial chamber. In addition to putting sociological data to political use, there must be a concern with the education of men in the process of living together.

Buber's entire sociology is of a piece with his philosophy and theology in placing central stress on the concept of the *community (Gemeinschaft)*. For him this was not an ideal type or conceptual construction as in some of the systems of German sociology like those of Toennies or Max Weber. It was an empirical type of society with certain marked features — notably a serious and constant concern with the relationship of the divine in the manifestations of routine living. The establishment of such a social organization was in profound consonance with the doctrine of Judaism that the ideal is always the outflowing of real, natural urges and drives, and the ideal service of God is the establishment of the truly human community. For man's commitment to God must be manifested not in solemn ritual and world-rejecting meditation but in daily living. The Judaistic doctrine of unification permits of no dualism as between the ethics of the individual and the state, or between the life of religion and life in the world.

Apparently credit must go to Ferdinand Toennies, the founder of German sociology, for making the fundamental distinction between community which deriving from *communio* signifies an organic, deep seated, emotionally pervasive and hence genuine form of living together, as opposed to society or association which is more mechanical, temporary, purposive, and hence artificial or ephemeral. Indeed, Toennies speaks as though a *Gemeinschaft* was itself an organism when contrasted with the artificial character of society.

From this doctrine of *Gemeinschaft* both Landauer and Buber developed their philosophy of the community — as the highest form of human symbiosis. This philosophy of community was influenced by but was also in part a protest against Marxism.

Buber construes the essence of community as being identical with the *Bund* and not, as in Toennies' view, with the natural community of the family or village — a free association of individuals who find one another in direct relationship, or an elective community of those who cluster about a religious center. He espouses the rebirth of the commune or the cooperative but he does not undertake to solve the technical questions as to the degree of economic or political autonomy to be permitted these cooperatives or communes, nor in general to lay down general principles as to the relation between centralization and decentralization. This massive problem, Buber avers, must be approached, like everything having to do with the relationship between idea and reality, only with great spiritual tact, with a constant and tireless weighing and measuring of the right proportion between them. He insists, however, that the community process and attitude must determine the relations of the communes with each other, for only "a community of communities merits the title of Commonwealth."

In its positive conclusion, then, this work is a plea for a renewal and deepening of the Cooperative movement,[1] with its drive toward the structural renewal of society, the re-establishment of inward social relationships within it, and the emergence of new congeries of communitarian states (*consociatio consociationum*). This trend, far from being romantic or utopian, is, rather, constructive to the highest degree. What is necessary is not merely cooperative organization of production or consumption, but the comprehensive integral "full cooperative," the most potent manifestation of which is the village commune, "where communal living is based on the amalgamation of production and consumption, production being understood not exclusively as agriculture alone, but as the organic union of agriculture with industry and handicrafts."

It may be helpful to recall that Buber had affiliations,

---

[1] Buber's survey of the cooperative movement takes its place with the works of Gide, Infield, Mladenatz, Kropotkin, and Kaznelson.

both personal and ideological, with the religious-socialist movement in Germany — a variegated manifestation of concern with the social gospel which after World War I culminated in an outright effort at a synthesis of religion and socialism. Under the impact of modern social problems, religion, particularly Protestant Christianity, endeavored to find satisfactory solutions for the many aspects of social disorganization induced by the rapid and unregulated development of capitalism. Thus the Protestant churches of Germany and Switzerland, particularly, developed a noteworthy social-religious trend, and both they and the Roman Church endeavored to find ways of reaching the proletariat, which had become increasingly alienated from the churches. One aspect of this trend led to the formation of the Christian Social Party, headed by the demogogic preacher Stoecker, while the Protestant churches developed a program which crystallized in the formation of the Evangelical Social Congress. There was also a more liberal religious group which had a different attitude toward socialism than the Protestant and Roman churches. For the Christian Social Party was conservative in both theology and in politics and in sharp opposition to the Social Democratic Party. On the other hand, the Evangelical Social Party had a liberal orientation both politically and theologically, and their rejection of socialism was by no means as emphatic as that of the Christian Socialists. But in the freer Social Religious Movement there was a positive attitude manifested toward the Social Democratic Party, especially in its radical attack upon the bourgeois social order. Finally, there was to emerge, after World War I, a Religious Socialist group.

The source of this freer German social gospel movement has been traced to the work of two distinguished German pietistic preachers, Johann Christoph Blumhardt and his son Christoph, whose influence later spread from Germany to Switzerland. Two other men also deserve credit for having developed a socially conscious religious perspective. One was Hermann Kutter (who died in 1931), who in a series of prophetic critiques of the church of his time expounded the view that God had willed to manifest Himself in the atheistic and materialistic Social Democratic Party because it was doing the work which Christianity ought properly to have done. Never politically active nor a member of the Socialist Party, he was zealous for God and social justice, and he interpreted the socialistic movement as a sign of God's wrath against His own peole, whom He had abandoned in order to shame the pious by consorting with the godless. The other great spokesman for the social religious movement in Switzerland was Leonhard Ragaz (who died in 1948), and who, unlike Kutter, had a very definite program of social reform for which he fought throughout his life. He also differed from Kutter in his unceasing effort to produce a synthesis of Christianity and socialism. He averred that he was a member of the Social Democratic Party because he saw in it something of the Kingdom of God and the adumbration of the Christian truth. In the socialist ideal he saw a new world of solidarity supplanting a world of brigandage, and a new hegemony of the spirit in place of the dominion of matter; man was to be in the ascendant rather than mammon; service rather than power.

The culmination of this synthesis was a religious socialism of which Ragaz may properly be regarded as the founder. Under his influence there was already in existence in Switzerland prior to World War I a society of Social Democratic ministers who led groups of Social Democratic churchmen, and the religious socialism spread to Germany after World War I. One of its manifestations was the endeavor to bring together the working class and the church by affirmation of socialism on the part of Christian leaders. There was a small group of intellectuals who gathered around men like Paul Tillich, Karl Mennicke and Eduard Heimann, whose main concern was to deepen the religious level of socialism for the purpose of enabling it, once it had achieved this deeper level of understanding, to produce or generate the desiderated "theonomous era," as Tillich termed it. Indeed, the latter continued to be one of the leading spirits in the religious socialist movement and perhaps its most sophisticated ideologist, writing widely on the subject and contributing to the authoritative German encyclopedia of religion, *Die Religion in Geschichte und Gegenwart*, the significant article on religious socialism. He interpreted this movement not as the religious absolutization of the socialist movement, but, rather, as a protest against the absolutization of the middle class and the contemporary social order; he also admitted that it constituted a recognition of the problems inescapably brought to the attention of modern man by sociology. The social and ethical ideal of religious socialism, he declared, is the achievement of a meaningful and thoroughly reasonable society in which the concrete potentiality of other human beings comes to recognition or, what amounts to the same, in which true community arises. Religious socialism was for Tillich the quest for a new social and cultural existence filled with transcendant content (theonomy).

The situation was quite different in the various societies of "religious socialists" that arose in Germany after 1919. Most of these groups were led by ministers and had the double purpose of combatting the dominant atheism in the Social Democratic Party in favor of a more sympathetic attitude toward Christianity and of creating in the church a positive understanding of socialism. Of course the religious socialists were not Marxists, though no one can doubt their socialism. But it was of the "utopian" variety which Marx had so scornfully dismissed in his *Communist Manifesto*. In January, 1919, there came into being in Berlin a "Society of Socialistic Friends of the Church" which a year later took the name of "Society of Religious Socialists." This had many sections in Berlin and local groups in such cities as Cologne, Stettin, Breslau and Koenigsberg, but at the height of its popularity it had not many more than two thousand members. There were other comparable groups independent of the Berlin society, as for example in Baden. In 1924 the various societies joined forces and in 1926 took the name "Society of Religious Socialists of Germany." They began to issue a significant journal, *Zeitschrift für Religion und Sozialismus,* edited by Professor Georg Wuensch of Marburg. The movement was of course terminated immediately after the victory of the Nationalist Socialist Party.

If one inquires as to the influence of this movement of religious socialism, one is bound to say that it was not very effective. The Social Democratic Party tolerated it but scarcely advanced it, and the working class was very little touched by it. On the other hand the religious socialist group was suspect to the churches and the organizations connected with them, and it failed in its desired aim of inducing a more friendly judgment of socialism among church people. It would appear that religious socialism lacked the evangelical fervor which might have achieved noteworthy popular influence. The various constituent units manifested little of the pietistic quality of the Blumhardts, Kutter, or Ragaz. Most of the leaders belonged to the liberal theological wing and were rather close to the very free religious groups, having but little understanding of the nature and function of the church. As it turned out, their criticism of the church was very sharp, while their judgment of the failings of the socialist movement was rather muted. Their endeavor to achieve a synthesis between socialism and Christianity frequently led them to equate socialist slogans with Christian ones, thus identifying the classless society with the Kingdom of God and the class struggle with the Holy War. There was the ever-present danger that the religious content might become completely secularized.

But for all the criticisms that were leveled at the religious socialist movement on the part of the churches, there can be no doubt that it contributed much to freeing the church from its excessively close connection with the bourgeoisie and nationalism. In this respect the achievements of Kutter and Ragaz had a permanent value.

After World War II the religious socialist movement arose anew on a small scale. Once again there is a society of German religious socialists with a central office in Frankfurt, and the organization issues a periodical entitled *Christ*

und Sozialist. Apparently the present society is much closer
to the church than the previous ones, and its leaders obviously have a stronger theological foundation and back-
ground. Nor is there as strong a polemic against the
church as in the earlier decade. Rather there appears to
be a genuine effort to achieve a clearer understanding between the church and the working class through the dia-
logue between these two great forces.

Sombre indeed is Buber's appraisal of the present situation, yet he is hopeful. He sees great forces arrayed against
one another, yet he is confident of a messianic amelioration.
One of the nineteenth-century mappers of a path to Utopia
was Moses Hess, for whom Buber had a high regard. In one
of his works, *Rome and Jerusalem,* Hess assigned a unique
function to Israel in the modern world. Following this
example, Buber sets up a contrast at this moment of history between Moscow and Jerusalem:

> So long as Russia has not undergone an essential
> inner change — and today we have no means of know-
> ing when and how that will come to pass — we must
> designate one of the two poles of Socialism between
> which our choice lies, by the formidable name of
> "Moscow." The other, I would make bold to call
> "Jerusalem."

Indeed, the words in which Buber characterizes Hess
(*Israel and Palestine,* pp. 112f.) apply equally to his own
views:

> Much as he recognizes the importance of social
> conditions for the development of social ideas, he
> nevertheless considers it essential that socialism should
> be based not on the economic and technical stage of
> development alone but also on that of the spirit. For
> him social freedom is either a result of spiritual free-
> dom, or it is without foundation and turns over into
> its opposite; he sees the heart of the social movements
> of our time proceeding "not from the needs of the
> stomach but from the needs of the heart" and from
> "ideas."

He does not retreat from the insight into the importance of material conditions for the development of social ends, but goes beyond it. And in two ways. On the one hand he is concerned to fit socialism into a wider supra-social cosmic content — and not into a materialistically grounded context but following on from Spinoza . . . into harmonious conformity to a law which manifests itself in different spheres, the cosmic, the organic, the practical and the social, without any possibility of deriving one from the other.

In speaking of the saintly Rabbi Kook (*Israel and Palestine*, p. 148), Buber again employs language descriptive of his own stand:

Fundamentally he is not concerned so much with the continuation of the existing holiness as with a true renewal. And for him holiness means not a sphere above life, but the renewal of life and unity and the transfiguration of this wholeness and unity.

What is the reaction of a social scientist to Buber's noble ideological analysis of utopianism?

From the viewpoint of social science, Henrik Infield, an empirical observer of communitarian experiments and one who has also been stimulated by the *Kvutza* (*cf.* his *Cooperative Living in Palestine*, 1948), expresses a certain discontent with the philosophical rehabilitation of utopia. Agreeing that a reassessment of utopian thought is desirable, he questions the value of an ideological analysis in terms of absolutes, even though Marxism has been proved wrong, and argues that a return to utopia is impossible. There may be other alternatives than utopian socialism; e.g., single tax; and the criteria of the good society may well change. Actually he goes on to challenge the radical distinctions of the either/or variety postulated by Buber in regard to the difference between utopian, and scientific socialism. For there are utopian and apocalyptic traits in scientific socialism and the converse is also true, at least in part. Science and utopia are not mutually exclusive propositions, so that despair of the former need not necessarily drive us to the latter. For the social scientist, Infield stresses, the reification of state and society and the absolutization of ideals are barriers to critical investigation of societal phenomena. Indeed, there is no reason to question Infield's concern with an experimental approach to social problems — and his preoccupation with precise methods and techniques for investigation. Cooperative communities certainly are important socio-economic laboratories for our time; and it is to be hoped that the International Council for Research in the Sociology for Cooperation will undertake and support research in the sociological problems of all types of cooperatives, and that its International Library for the Sociology for Cooperation will publish these findings.

Infield's impatience with philosophical analysis of fundamental problems leads him to doubt the value of the term "utopian" altogether, and he identifies it with a eulogistic term suggesting praise of a social deviation. For Buber this is to neglect the basic distinction between *Gemeinschaft* and *Gesellschaft* types of society. Whatever the force of the impatient dismissal by empirical researchers of such fundamental conceptual inquiries as are contained in this work, we are enriched by this fresh exploration of the eternal problems of social philosophy and practice. We remain in the debt of Buber for proclaiming afresh to our generation the message of Leonhard Ragaz: "Any Socialism which sets limits to God and man is too narrow for me."

In a brief essay on "Three Theses of a Religious Socialism" which is introduced by the above quotation, Buber affirms anew his faith in messianic or prophetic socialism. In defining religious socialism he stresses that religion and socialism are dependent on one another, and that each of them needs the covenant with the other for the fulfillment and perfection of its own essence. *"Religio*, that is, the human person's binding of himself to God, can only attain its full reality in the will for a community of the human race, out of which alone God can prepare His kingdom."

Attachment to God and community among human beings belong together: "Religion without socialism is disembodied spirit, and hence not authentic spirit; socialism without religion is body emptied of spirit, hence also not genuine body.

"All 'socialist' tendencies, programs and parties are real or fictitious according to whether they serve as the strength, direction, and instruments of real *socialitas* — of mankind's really becoming a fellowship — or whether they only exist alongside its development, or even conceal the flight from real *socialitas,* which comprises men's immediate living with and for one another in the here and now."

Buber emphasizes that the point where religion and socialism can meet is in the "concrete personal life." He maintains that in both the stress is properly on the *inward aspect.* In religion this means that dogma and ritual are secondary to abiding in the profundity of a "real reciprocal relation with the mystery of God." Similarly the heart of socialism's truth is not any tenet or political strategy but an enduring orientation "in the abyss of concrete reciprocal relation with the mystery of man."

Buber holds that it is presumptuous to expect to accomplish socialism without living out a communitarian pattern. As in religion it is the management of the workaday world "that sanctifies or desecrates religious devotion," so in socialism there must be a constant concern with the means employed to secure its ends lest the goals be vitiated or impugned by the means. For in religious socialism the most serious attention is given to certain fundamental existential facts: "the fact that God is, that the world is, and that the concrete human person stands before God and in the world."

EPHRAIM FISCHOFF

I

THE IDEA

AMONG the sections of the Communist Manifesto which have exerted the most powerful influence on the generations up to our own day is that entitled "Der kritisch-utopistische Sozialismus und Kommunismus" (The Critical-Utopian Socialism and Communism).

Marx and Engels were entrusted by the "League of the Just" with the formulation of a communist credo—an important preliminary to the convocation of a Universal Communist Congress, the "Union of all the Oppressed", planned for 1848. The League Directorate laid down that fundamental expression should also be given in this credo to the "position as regards the socialist and communist parties", i.e. the line of demarcation dividing the League from the affiliated movements, by which were meant above all the Fourierists, "those shallow folk" as they are called in the draft of the credo which the Central Authority presented to the London League Congress. In the draft written by Engels there is as yet no mention of "utopian" socialists or communists; we hear only of people who put forward "superlative systems of reform", "who, on the pretext of reorganizing society, want to bolster up the foundation of existing society and consequently the society itself," and who are therefore described as "bourgeois socialists" to be attacked—a description which, in the final version, applies in particular to Proudhon. The distance between the Engels draft and the final version drawn up substantially by Marx is immense.

The "systems", of which those of Saint-Simon, Fourier and Owen are mentioned (in Marx's original version Cabet, Weitling and even Babeuf are also named as authors of such systems), are all described as the fruit of an epoch in which industry was not yet developed and hence the "proletariat" problem was not yet grasped; instead there appeared those same systems which could not be other than fictitious, fantastic and utopian, whose aim was at bottom to abolish that very class-conflict which was only just beginning to take shape and from which the "universal transformation of society" would ultimately proceed. Marx was here formulating afresh what he had said shortly before in his polemic against Proudhon: "These theoreticians are Utopians; they are driven to seek science in their own heads, because things are not yet so far advanced that they need only give an account of what is happening under their eyes and make themselves its instruments." The criticism of existing conditions on which the systems are built is recognized as valuable explanatory material; on the other hand all their positive recommendations are condemned to lose all practical value and theoretical justification in the course of historical development.

We can only assess the political character of this declaration in the framework of the socialist-communist movement of the time when we realize that it was directed against the views which used to reign in the "League of the Just" itself and were supplanted by Marx's ideas. Marx characterized these views twelve years after the appearance of the Communist Manifesto as a "secret doctrine" consisting of a "hodge-podge of Anglo-French socialism or communism and German philosophy", and to this he opposed his "scientific insight into the economic structure of bourgeois society as the only tenable theoretical basis". The point now, he says, was to show that it "was not a matter of bringing some utopian system or other into being but of consciously participating in the historical revolutionary process of society that was taking place before our eyes". The polemical or anti-utopian section of the Manifesto thus signifies an internal political action in the strictest sense: the victorious conclusion of the struggle which Marx, with Engels at his side, had waged against the other so-called—or self-styled—communist movements, primarily in the "League of the Just" itself (which was now christened the "League of Communists"). The concept "utopian" was the last and most pointed shaft which he shot in this fray.

I have just said: "with Engels at his side." Nevertheless reference should not be omitted to a number of passages from the Introduction with which Engels, some two years before the Manifesto was drafted, had prefaced his translation of a fragment from the posthumous writings of Fourier. Here, too, he speaks of those same doctrines which are dismissed as utopian in the Manifesto; here, too, Fourier, Saint-Simon and Owen are quoted; here, too, a distinction is made in their works between the valuable criticism of existing society and the far less relevant "schematization" of a future one; but earlier on he says: "What the French and the English were saying ten, twenty, even forty years ago—and saying very well, very clearly, in very fine language—is at long last, and in fragmentary fashion, becoming known to the Germans, who have been 'hegelizing' it for the past year or at best re-discovering it after the event and bringing it out in a much worse and more abstract form as a wholly new discovery." And Engels adds word for word: "I make no exception even of my own works." The struggle thus touched his own past. Still more important, though, is the following pronouncement: "Fourier constructs the future for himself after having correctly recognized the past and present." This must be weighed against the charges which the Manifesto lays at the door of utopianism. Nor should we forget that the Manifesto was written only ten years after Fourier's death.

What Engels says thirty years after the Manifesto in his book against Dühring about these self-same "three great Utopians", and what passed with a few additions into the influential publication *The Evolution of Socialism from Utopia to Science* a little later, is merely an elaboration of the points already made in the Manifesto. It is immediately striking that once again only the same three men, "the founders of Socialism", are discussed, those very people who were "utopians", "because they could not be anything else at a time when capitalist production was so little developed", people who were compelled "to construct the elements of a new society out of their heads because these elements had not yet become generally visible in the old society". In the thirty years between the Manifesto and the anti-Dühring book had no socialists emerged who, in Engels' opinion, deserved the epithet "utopians" and his notice alike, but who could not be conceded those extenuating circumstances, since in their day the economic conditions were already developed and "the social tasks" no longer "hidden"? To name only one and of course the greatest—Proudhon—one of whose earlier books, *The Economic Contradictions or the Philosophy of Misery*, Marx had attacked in his famous Polemic written before the Manifesto—from Proudhon a series of important works had appeared meanwhile which no scientific theory about the social situation and the social tasks could afford to overlook; did he also (from whose book, albeit attacked by Marx, the Communist Manifesto had at any rate borrowed the concept of the "socialist utopia") belong to the Utopians, but to those who could not be justified? True, in the Manifesto he had been named as an example of the "conservative or bourgeois socialists" and in the Polemic Marx had declared that Proudhon was far inferior to the socialists, "because he has neither sufficient courage nor sufficient insight to raise himself, if only speculatively, above the bourgeois horizon"; and after Proudhon's death he asseverated in a public obituary that even to-day he would have to confirm every word of this judgment, and a year later he explained in a letter that Proudhon had done "immense harm" and, by his "sham-criticism and sham-opposition to the Utopians" had corrupted the younger generation and the workers. But another year later, nine years before writing the anti-Dühring book, Engels states in one of the seven reviews which he published anonymously on the first volume of Marx's *Capital*, that Marx wanted to "provide socialist strivings with the scientific foundation which neither Fourier nor Proudhon nor even Lassalle had been able to give" —from which there clearly emerges the rank he awarded to Proudhon despite everything.

In 1844 Marx and Engels (in their book *The Holy Family*) had found in Proudhon's book on Property a scientific advance which "revolutionizes political economy and makes a science of political economy possible for the first time"; they had further declared that not only did he write in the interests of the proletariat but that he was a proletarian himself and his work "a scientific manifesto of the French proletariat" of historic significance. And as late as May, 1846, in an anonymous essay, Marx had dubbed him "a communist", in a context, moreover, which makes it obvious that Proudhon was still a representative communist in his eyes at the time, some six months before the Polemic was written. What had happened in the meantime to move Marx to so radical an alteration of his judgment? Certainly, Proudhon's "Contradictions" had appeared, but this book in no way represented a decisive modification of Proud-hon's views, also the violent diatribe against communist (by which Proudhon means what we would call "collectivist") Utopias is only a more detailed elaboration of his criticism of

the "Communauté" which can be read in the first discussion
on property, so lauded by Marx, in 1840. However, Proudhon's
refusal of Marx's invitation of collaboration had preceded the
"Contradictions". The situation becomes clearer for us when
we read what Marx wrote to Engels in July, 1870, after the
outbreak of war: "The French need a thrashing. If the
Prussians win, the centralization of State power will subserve
the centralization of the German working-class. German
domination would furthermore shift the focus of the Western-
European workers' movement from France to Germany, and
you have merely to compare the movement in the two countries
from 1866 up to now to see that the German working-class is
superior both in theory and in organization to the French.
Its supremacy over that of the French on the world-stage would
at once mean the supremacy of *our* theory over Proudhon's, etc."
It is thus in eminent degree a matter of *political* attitude. Hence
it must be regarded as consistent that Engels should describe
Proudhon soon afterwards in a polemic against him (*On the
Housing Question*) as a pure dilettante, facing economics
helplessly and without knowledge, one who preaches and
laments "where we offer proofs". At the same time Proudhon
is clearly labelled a Utopian: the "best world" he constructs is
already "crushed in the bud by the foot of onward-marching
industrial development".

I have dwelt on this topic at some length because something
of importance can best be brought to light in this way.
Originally Marx and Engels called those people Utopians
whose thinking had preceded the critical development of
industry, the proletariat and the class-war, and who therefore
could not take this development into account; subsequently
the term was levelled indiscriminately at all those who, in the
estimation of Marx and Engels, did not in fact take account
of it; and of these the late-comers either did not understand
how to do so or were unwilling or both. The epithet "Utopian"
thereafter became the most potent missile in the fight of
Marxism against non-Marxian socialism. It was no longer a
question of demonstrating the rightness of one's own opinion
in the face of a contrary one; in general one found science and
truth absolutely and exclusively in his own position and
utopianism and delusion in the rival camp. To be a "Utopian"
in our age means: to be out of step with modern economic
development, and what modern economic development is we

learn of course from Marxism. Of those "pre-historic" Utopians, Saint-Simon, Fourier and Owen, Engels had declared in his *German Peasant War in 1850* that German socialist theory would never forget that it stood on the shoulders of these men, "who despite all their fantasticalness and all their utopianism must be counted among the most significant brains of all time, who anticipated with genius countless truths whose validity we can now prove scientifically".

But here again—and this is consistent from the political point of view—consideration is no longer given to the possibility that there are men living today, known and unknown, who anticipate truths whose validity will be scientifically proved in the future, truths which contemporary "science"—i.e. the trend of knowledge which not infrequently identifies itself in general with Science—is determined to regard as invalid, exactly as was the case with those "founders of socialism" in their day. They were Utopians as forerunners, these are Utopians as obscurantists. They blazed the trail for Science, these obstruct it. Happily, however, it is sufficient to brand them Utopians to render them innocuous.

Perhaps I may be allowed to cite a small personal experience as an instance of this method of "annihilation by labels". In Whitsun, 1928, there took place in my former home-town of Heppenheim a discussion,[1] attended mainly by delegates from religious socialist circles, on the question of how to nourish anew those spiritual forces of mankind on which the belief in a renewal of society rests. In my speech, in which I laid particular emphasis on the generally neglected and highly concrete questions of decentralization and the status of the worker, I said: "It is of no avail to call 'utopian' what we have not yet tested with our powers." That did not save me from a critical remark on the part of the Chairman, who simply relegated me to the ranks of utopian socialists and left it at that.

But if socialism is to emerge from the blind-alley into which it has strayed, among other things the catchword "Utopian" must be cracked open and examined for its true content.

---

[1] The minutes appeared in Zurich 1929 under the title "Sozialismus aus dem Glauben" (Socialism from Faith).

II

THE UTOPIAN
ELEMENT IN SOCIALISM

WHAT, at first sight, seems common to the Utopias that have
passed into the spiritual history of mankind, is the fact that
they are pictures, and pictures moreover of something not
actually present but only represented. Such pictures are
generally called fantasy-pictures, but that tells us little enough.
This "fantasy" does not float vaguely in the air, it is not driven
hither and thither by the wind of caprice, it centres with
architectonic firmness on something primary and original
which it is its destiny to build; and this primary thing is a wish.
The utopian picture is a picture of what "should be", and the
visionary is one who wishes it to be. Therefore some call the
Utopias wish-pictures, but that again does not tell us enough. A
"wish-picture" makes us think of something that rises out of the
depths of the Unconscious and, in the form of a dream, a
reverie, a "seizure", overpowers the defenceless soul, or may,
at a later stage, even be invoked, called forth, hatched out by
the soul itself. In the history of the human spirit the image-
creating wish—although it, too, like all image-making is rooted
deep down in us—has nothing instinctive about it and nothing
of self-gratification. It is bound up with something supra-
personal that communes with the soul but is not governed
by it. What is at work here is the longing for that *rightness*
which, in religious or philosophical vision, is experienced as
revelation or idea, and which of its very nature cannot be
realized in the individual, but only in human community.
The vision of "what should be"—independent though it may
sometimes appear of personal will—is yet inseparable from
a critical and fundamental relationship to the existing condition of humanity. All suffering under a social order that is
senseless prepares the soul for vision, and what the soul re-

ceives in this vision strengthens and deepens its insight into the perversity of what is perverted. The longing for the realization of "the seen" fashions the picture.

The vision of rightness in Revelation is realized in the picture of a perfect time—as messianic eschatology; the vision of rightness in the Ideal is realized in the picture of a perfect space—as Utopia. The first necessarily goes beyond the social and borders on the creational, the cosmic; the second necessarily remains bounded by the circumference of society, even if the picture it presents sometimes implies an inner transformation of man. Eschatology means perfection of creation; Utopia the unfolding of the possibilities, latent in mankind's communal life, of a "right" order. Another difference is still more important. For eschatology the decisive act happens from above, even when the elemental or prophetic form of it gives man a significant and active share in the coming redemption; for Utopia everything is subordinated to conscious human will, indeed we can characterize it outright as a picture of society designed as though there were no other factors at work than conscious human will. But they are neither of them mere cloud castles: if they seek to stimulate or intensify in the reader or listener his critical relationship to the present, they also seek to show him perfection—in the light of the Absolute, but at the same time as something towards which an active path leads from the present. And what may seem impossible as a concept arouses, as an image, the whole might of faith, ordains purpose and plan. It does this because it is in league with powers latent in the depths of reality. Eschatology, in so far as it is prophetic, Utopia, in so far as it is philosophical, both have the character of realism.

The Age of Enlightenment and its aftermath robbed religious eschatology in increasing measure of its sphere of action: in the course of ten generations it has become more and more difficult for man to believe that at some point in the future an act from above will redeem the human world, i.e. transform it from a senseless one into one full of meaning, from disharmony into harmony. This incapacity has become an actual physical incapacity, in avowedly religious no less than in a-religious people, save that in the former it is concealed from consciousness by the fixed nexus of tradition. On the other hand, the age of technology with its growing social contradictions has influenced Utopia profoundly. Under the influence of pan-technical trends Utopia too has become wholly technical; conscious human will, its foundation hitherto, is now understood as technics, and society like Nature is to be mastered by technological calculation and construction. Society, however, with its present contradictions poses a question that cannot be dismissed; all thinking and planning for the future must seek the answer to it, and where Utopia is concerned the political and cultural formulations necessarily give way before the task of contriving a "right" order of society. But here social thinking shows its superiority over technical thinking. Utopias which revel in technical fantasias mostly find foothold nowadays only in the feebler species of novel, in which little or none of the imagination that went into the grand Utopias of old can be discovered. Those, on the contrary, which undertake to deliver a blueprint of the perfect social structure, turn into systems. But into these "utopian" social systems there enters all the force of dispossessed Messianism. The social system of modern socialism or communism has, like eschatology, the character of an annunciation or of a proclamation. It is true that Plato was moved by the desire to establish a reality proportioned to the Idea, and it is true that he also sought, to the end of his days and with unflagging passion, for the human tools of its realization; but only with the modern social systems did there arise this fierce interplay of doctrine and action, planning and experiment. For Thomas More it was still possible to mingle serious instruction with incongruous jesting, and, with supercilious irony, to allow a picture of "very absurd" institutions to rub shoulders with such as he "wishes rather than hopes" to see copied. For Fourier that was no longer possible; here everything is practical inference and logical resolve, for the point with him is "to emerge at last from a civilization which, far from being man's social destiny, is only mankind's childhood sickness".

The polemics of Marx and Engels have resulted in the term "utopian" becoming used, both within Marxism and without, for a socialism which appeals to reason, to justice, to the will of man to remedy the maladjustments of society, instead of his merely acquiring an active awareness of what is "dialectically" brewing in the womb of industrialism. All voluntaristic socialism is rated "utopian". Yet it is by no means the case that the socialism diametrically opposed to it—which we may call necessitarian because it professes to demand nothing more than the setting in motion of the necessary evolutionary machinery—is free of utopianism. The utopian elements in it are of another kind and stand in a different context.

I have already indicated that the whole force of dispossessed eschatology was converted into Utopia at the time of the French Revolution. But, as I have intimated, there are two basic forms of eschatology: the prophetic, which at any given moment sees every person addressed by it as endowed, in a degree not to be determined beforehand, with the power to participate by his decisions and deeds in the preparing of Redemption: and the apocalyptic, in which the redemptive process in all its details, its very hour and course, has been fixed from everlasting and for whose accomplishment human beings are only used as tools, though what is immutably fixed may yet be "unveiled" to them, revealed, and they be assigned their function. The first of these forms derives from Israel, the second from ancient Persia. The differences and agreements between the two, their combinations and separations, play an important part in the inner history of Christianity. In the socialist secularization of eschatology they work out separately: the prophetic form in some of the systems of the so-called Utopians, the apocalyptic one above all in Marxism (which is not to say that no prophetic element is operative here—it has only been overpowered by the apocalyptic). With Marx, belief in humanity's road through contradiction to the overcoming of the same, takes the form of Hegelian dialectic, since he makes use of a scientific inquiry into the changing processes of production; but the vision of upheavals past or to come "in the chain of absolute necessity", as Hegel says, does not derive from Hegel. Marx's apocalyptic position is purer and stronger than Hegel's, which lacked any real driving power for the future; Franz Rosenzweig has pointed out, and rightly, that Marx remained truer to Hegel's belief in historical determinism than Hegel himself. "No one else has seen so directly where and how and in what form the last day would dawn on the horizon of history." The point at which, in Marx, the utopian apocalypse breaks out and the whole topic of economics and science is transformed into pure "utopics", is the convulsion of all things *after* the social revolution. The Utopia of the so-called Utopians is pre-revolutionary, the Marxist one post-revolutionary. The "withering away" of the State, "the leap of humanity out of the realm of necessity into the realm of freedom" may be well-founded dialectically, but it is no longer so scientifically. As a Marxist thinker, Paul Tillich, says, these things "can in no way be made intelligible in terms of existing reality", "between reality and expectation there is a gulf", "for this reason Marxism has never, despite its animosity to Utopias, been able to clear itself of the suspicion of a hidden belief in Utopia". Or in the words of another Marxist sociologist, Eduard Heimann: "With men as they are, a withering away of the State is inconceivable. In speculating on a radical and inmost change of human nature, we pass beyond the borders of empirical research and enter the realm of prophetic vision where the true significance and providential destination of man are circumscribed in stammering metaphors." But what is of decisive significance for us is the difference between this Utopianism and that of the non-marxist socialists. We shall have to observe this difference more closely.

When we examine what Marxist criticism calls the utopian element in the non-marxist systems; we find that it is by no means simple or uniform. Two distinct elements are to be distinguished. The essence of one is schematic fiction, the essence of the other is organic planning. The first, as we encounter it particularly in Fourier, originates in a kind of abstract imagination which, starting from a theory of the nature of man, his capacities and needs, deduces a social order that shall employ all his capacities and satisfy all his needs. Although in Fourier the theory is supported by a mass of observational material, every observation becomes unreal and untrustworthy as soon as it enters this sphere; and in his social order, which pretends to be social architecture but is in reality formless schematism, all problems (as Fourier himself says) have the same "solution", that is, from real problems in the life of human beings they become artificial problems in the life of instinctive robots—artificial problems which all allow of the same solution because they all proceed from the same mechanistic set-up. Wholly different, indeed of a directly contrary nature, is the second element. Here the dominant purpose is to inaugurate, from an impartial and undogmatic understanding of contemporary man and his condition, a transformation of both, so as to overcome the contradictions which make up the essence of our social order.

Starting with no reservations from the condition of society as it is, this view gazes into the depths of reality with a clarity of vision unclouded by any dogmatic pre-occupation, discerning those still hidden tendencies which, although obscured by more obvious and more powerful forces, are yet moving towards that transformation. It has justly been said that in a positive sense every planning intellect is utopian. But we must add that the planning intellect of the socialist "Utopians" under consideration, proves the positive character of its utopianism by being at every point aware, or at least having an inkling, of the diversity, indeed the contrariety, of the trends discernible in every age; by not failing to discover, despite its insight into the dominant trends, those others which these trends conceal; and by asking whether and to what extent those and those alone are aiming at an order in which the contradictions of existing society will truly be overcome.

Here, then, we have one or two motives which require further explanation and amplification both in themselves and in order to mark them off from Marxism.

In the course of the development of so-called utopian socialism its leading representatives have become more and more persuaded that neither the social problem nor its solution can be reduced to a lowest common denominator, and that every simplification—even the most intellectually important— exerts an unfavourable influence both on knowledge and action. When in 1846, some six months before he started his controversy with Proudhon, Marx invited the latter to collaborate with him in a "correspondence" which should sub- serve "an exchange of ideas and impartial criticism", and for which—so Marx writes—"as regards France we all believe that we could find no better correspondent than yourself," he received the answer: "Let us, if you wish, look together for the laws of society, the manner in which they are realized, but after we have cleared away all these a priori dogmatisms, let us not, for God's sake, think of tangling people up in doctrines in our turn! Let us not fall into the contradiction of your countryman Martin Luther who, after having overthrown the catholic theology, immediately set about founding a protestant theology of his own amid a great clamour of excommunications and anathemas. . . . Because we stand in the van of a new move- ment let us not make ourselves the protagonists of a new intolerance, let us not act like apostles of a new religion, even if it be a religion of logic, a religion of reason." Here it is chiefly a question of political means, but from many of Proudhon's utterances it is evident that he saw the ends as well in the light of the same freedom and diversity. And fifty years after that letter Kropotkin summed up the basic view of the ends in a single sentence: the fullest development of individuality "will combine with the highest development of voluntary association in all its aspects, in all possible degrees and for all possible purposes; an association that is always changing, that bears in itself the elements of its own duration, that takes on the forms which best correspond at any given moment to the manifold strivings of all." This is precisely what Proudhon had wanted in the maturity of his thought. It may be contended that the Marxist objective is not essentially different in constitution; but at this point a yawning chasm opens out before us which can only be bridged by that special form of Marxist utopics, a chasm between, on the one side, the transformation to be consummated sometime in the future—no one knows how long after the final victory of the Revolution—and, on the other, the road to the Revolution and beyond it, which road is characterized by a far-reaching centralization that permits no individual features and no individual initiative. Uniformity as a means is to change miraculously into multiplicity as an end; compulsion into freedom. As against this the "utopian" or non-marxist socialist desires a means commensurate with his ends; he refuses to believe that in our reliance on the future "leap" we have to do now the direct opposite of what we are striving for; he believes rather that we must create here and now the space *now* possible for the thing for which we are striving, so that it may come to fulfilment *then*; he does not believe in the post-revolutionary leap, but he does believe in revolutionary continuity. To put it more precisely: he believes in a continuity within which revolution is only the accomplishment, the setting free and extension of a reality that has already grown to its true possibilities.

Seen from another angle this difference may be clarified still further. When we examine the capitalist society which has given birth to socialism, *as a society*, we see that it is a society inherently poor in structure and growing visibly poorer every day. By the structure of a society is to be understood its social content or community-content: a society can be called structurally rich to the extent that it is built up of genuine societies,

that is, local communes and trade communes and their step by
step association. What Gierke says of the Co-operative Movement in the Middle Ages is true of every structurally rich
society: it is "marked by a tendency to expand and extend the
unions, to produce larger associations over and above the
smaller association, confederations over and above individual
unions, all-embracing confederations over and above particular
confederations". At whatever point we examine the structure
of such a society we find the cell-tissue "Society" everywhere,
i.e. a living and life-giving collaboration, an essentially autonomous consociation of human beings, shaping and re-shaping
itself from within. Society is naturally composed not of
disparate individuals but of associative units and the associations between them. Under capitalist economy and the State
peculiar to it the constitution of society was being continually
hollowed out, so that the modern individualizing process
finished up as a process of atomization. At the same time the
old organic forms retained their outer stability, for the most
part, but they became hollow in sense and in spirit—a tissue of
decay. Not merely what we generally call the masses but the
whole of society is in essence amorphous, unarticulated, poor
in structure. Neither do those associations help which spring
from the meeting of economic or spiritual interests—the
strongest of which is the party: what there is of human intercourse in them is no longer a living thing, and the compensation
for the lost community-forms we seek in them can be found
in none. In the face of all this, which makes "society" a contradiction in terms, the "utopian" socialists have aspired more
and more to a restructuring of society; not, as the Marxist
critic thinks, in any romantic attempt to revive the stages of
development that are over and done with, but rather in
alliance with the decentralist counter-tendencies which can be
perceived underlying all economic and social evolution, and in
alliance with something that is slowly evolving in the human
soul: the most intimate of all resistances—resistance to mass or
collective loneliness.

Victor Hugo called Utopia "the truth of to-morrow".
Those efforts of the spirit, condemned as inopportune and
derided as "utopian socialism", may well be clearing the way
for the structure of society-to-be. (There is, of course, no
historical process that is necessary in itself and independent of
human resolve.) It is obvious that here, too, it is a matter of

preserving the community-forms that remain and filling them anew with spirit, and a new spirit. Over the gateway to Marxist centralization stands—for who knows how long?—the inscription in which Engels summed up the tyrannical character of the automatism in a great factory: "Lasciate ogni autonomia voi ch'entrate." Utopian socialism fights for the maximum degree of communal autonomy possible in a "restructured" society.

In that socialist meeting of 1928, I said: "There can be pseudo-realization of socialism, where the real life of man to man is but little changed. The real living together of man with man can only thrive where people have the real things of their common life in common; where they can experience, discuss and administer them together; where real fellowships and real work Guilds exist. We see more or less from the Russian attempt at realization that human relationships remain essentially unchanged when they are geared to a socialist-centralist hegemony which rules the life of individuals and the life of the natural social groups. Needless to say we cannot and do not want to go back to primitive agrarian communism or to the corporate State of the Christian Middle Ages. We must be quite unromantic, and, living wholly in the present, out of the recalcitrant material of our own day in history, fashion a true community."

III

THE FORERUNNERS

I HAVE pointed out that in "utopian" socialism there is an organically constructive and organically purposive or planning element which aims at a re-structuring of society, and moreover not at one that shall come to fruition in an indefinite future after the "withering away" of the proletarian dictatorstate, but beginning here and now in the given conditions of the present. If this is correct it should be possible to demonstrate, in the history of utopian socialism, the line of evolution taken by this element.

In the history of utopian socialism three pairs of active thinkers emerge, each pair being bound together in a peculiar way and also to its generation: Saint-Simon and Fourier, Owen and Proudhon, Kropotkin and Gustav Landauer. Through the middle pair there runs the line of cleavage separating the first phase of this socialism—the phase of transition to advanced capitalism—from the second, which accompanies the rise of the latter. In the first each thinker contributes a single constructive thought and these thoughts—at first strange and incompatible with one another—align themselves together, and in the second Proudhon and his successors build up the comprehensive synthesis, the synthetic idea of restructure. Each step occupies its own proper place and is not interchangeable.

A few figures will help to make the relations between the generations clear. Saint-Simon was born twelve years before Fourier and died twelve years before him, and yet both belong to the generation which was born before the French Revolution and perished before 1848—save that the younger, Fourier, belongs by nature and outlook to the eighteenth century and the older, Saint-Simon, to the nineteenth century. Owen was born before the great Revolution, Proudhon at the time of the Napoleonic triumphs; thus they belong congenitally to different generations but, as they both died between 1848 and 1870, death united them once more in a single generation. The same thing is repeated with Kropotkin, who was born before 1848, and Landauer, before 1870: both died soon after the first World War.

Saint-Simon—of whom the founder of sociology as a science, Lorenz von Stein, justly says that he " half understood, half guessed at *society*" (that is, society as such in contradistinction to the State) "for the first time in its full power, in all its elements and contradictions"—makes the first and, for his epoch, the most important contribution. The "puberty-crisis" which mankind had entered meant for him the eventual replacement of the existing régime by "le régime industriel". We can formulate it in this way: the cleavage of the social whole into two essentially different and mutually antagonistic orders is to yield place to a uniform structure. Hitherto society had been under a "government", now it was to come under an "administration", and the administration was not, like the former, to be entrusted to a class opposed to society and made up of "legalists" and "militarists", but to the natural leaders of society itself, the leaders of its production. No longer was one group of rulers to be ousted by another group of rulers, as had happened in all the upheavals known to history; what remains necessary as a police force does not constitute Government in the old sense. "The producers have no wish to be plundered by any one class of parasites rather than by any other. . . . It is clear that the struggle must end by being played out between the whole mass of parasites on the one hand and the mass of producers on the other, in order to decide whether the latter shall continue to be the prey of the former or shall obtain supreme control of society." Saint-Simon's naïve demand of "messieurs" the workers that they should make the entrepreneurs their leaders—a demand which was to weld the active portion of the capitalists and the proletarians into one class—contains, despite its odd air of unreality, the intimation of a future order in which no leadership is required other than that provided by the social functions themselves; in which politics have in fact become what they are in Saint-Simon's definition: "the science of production," i.e. of the pre-conditions most favourable to this. In the nature of things governments cannot implement policies of this sort; "government is a continual source of injury to industry when it meddles in its affairs; it is injurious even where it makes efforts to encourage it." Nothing but an overcoming of government as such can lead society out of the "extreme disorder" in which it languishes; out of the dilemma of a nation which is "essentially industrial" and whose government is "essentially feudal"; out of division into two classes: "one that orders and one that obeys" (the Saint-Simonist Bazard expressed it even more pungently soon after the death of his master, in 1829: "two classes, the exploiters and the exploited"). The present epoch is one of transition not from one sort of régime to another, but from a sham order to a true order, in which "work is the fountain-head of all virtues" and "the State is the confederacy of all workers" (so runs the formula of the Saint-Simonists). This cannot be the affair of a single nation only, for it would be opposed by other nations; the "industrial system" must be established over all Europe and the feudal system, persisting in bourgeois form, annihilated. Saint-Simon calls this "Europeanism". He realizes, however, that altering the relationship between the leaders and the led is not the sole intention, but that the alteration must permeate the whole inner structure of society. The moment when the industrial régime is "ripe" (i.e. when society is ripe for it can be "determined with reasonable exactitude by the fundamental circumstance that, in any given nation, the vast majority of individuals will by then have entered into more or less numerous industrial associations each two or three of which will be interconnected by industrial relationships. This will permit a general system to be built up, since the associations will be led towards a great common goal, as regards which they will be co-ordinated of themselves each according to its function". Here Saint-Simon comes very near to the idea of social re-structuring. What he lacks is the conception of genuine organic social units out of which this re-structuring can be built; the idea of "industrial associations" does not provide what is required. Saint-Simon divined the significance of the small social unit for the rebuilding of society, but did not recognize it for what it was.

It is just this social unit which is the be-all and end-all for Fourier. He thought he had discovered "the secret of association " and in this he saw—the formula dates from the same time, about 1820, when Saint-Simon gave his "industrial system" its final formulation—"the secret of the union of interests". Charles Gide has rightly pointed out that Fourier was here opposing the legacy of the French Revolution, which had contested the right of association and prohibited trades-unions; and opposing it because it was from the collapse of the cadres of the old corporations that the "anarchic" principle of free competition had derived, which, as Fourier's most important pupil—Considérant—had foretold in his manifesto of 1843 on the principles of socialism (by which the Communist Manifesto appears to have been influenced), would inevitably result in the exact opposite of what its introduction purposed, namely, in the "universal organization of great monopolies in all branches of industry". Fourier countered this with his "association communale sur le terrain de la production et de la consummation" (as Considérant again formulated it in 1848); which is to say the formation of local social units based on joint production and consumption. It is a new form of the "commune rurale", which latter is to be regarded as "l'élément alvéolaire de la société"—a conception not, of course, found in Fourier himself but only in his school that was also influenced by Owen (whom Fourier did not wish to read). Only free and voluntary association, so we are told in 1848, can solve the great organic problem of the future, "the problem of organizing a new order, an order in which individualism will combine spontaneously with 'collectism' " (sic). Only in this way can "the third and last emancipatory phase of history" come about, in which the first having made serfs out of slaves, and the second wage-earners out of serfs (we find this idea in Bazard as far back as 1829), "the abolition of the proletariat, the transformation of wage-earners into companions (associés)" will be accomplished. But one will scan Fourier's own expositions of his system and the drafts of his projects in vain for the concrete expression of his opposing principle. His "phalanstery" has been compared with a large hotel, and in fact it offers many similarities to those typical products of our age which meet the greatest possible part of their requirements with their own production—only that in this case production is managed by the guests themselves, and instead of the minimum conduct regulations as in the notices in hotel-rooms there is a law which regulates the daily round in all its details— a law that has various attractions and leaves one's powers of decision fundamentally untouched but is, in itself, meticulously exact. Although the supreme authority, the "Areopagus", issues no commands, but only gives instructions and each group acts according to its will, nevertheless this will simply "*cannot* deviate from that of the Areopagus, for he is the puissance d'opinion". Many things in this law may strike us as bizarre, but all the same it expresses some important and fruitful ideas, such as the alternation of various activities—a notion that foreshadows Kropotkin's "division of labour in time". On the other hand, and regarded precisely from this standpoint, the phalanstery is a highly unsocialistic institution. The division of labour in the course of a summer day leads the poor Lucas from the stables to the gardeners, from there to the reapers, the vegetable-growers, the manual workers, etc., while the same division of labour leads the rich Mondor from the "industrial parade" to the hunt, from there to fishing, to the library, greenhouses and so on. When we read that the poor have to enjoy a "graduated state of wealth that the rich may be happy", or that "only through the utmost inequality of worldly possessions can this beautiful and magnanimous agreement be reached", i.e. the renunciation by the rich of a great part of their dividends in favour of work and talent—we realize that these units which bear the stamp of a mechanical fantasy have no legitimate claim to be considered as the cells of a new and legitimate order. Their uniformity alone (for despite their appearance of inner diversity they represent, item for item, the same pattern, the same machinery) renders them totally unsuitable for a restructuring of society. Fourier's "universal harmony" which embraces world and society means, in society itself, only a harmony between the individuals living together, not a harmony between the units themselves (although some people may, of course, imagine a "federation of phalanges"). The interconnection between the units has no place in his system, each unit is a world on its own and always the same world; but of the attraction which rules the universe we hear nothing as between these units, they do not fuse together into associations, into higher units, indeed they cannot do so because they are not, like individuals, diversified, they do not complement one another and cannot therefore form a harmony. Fourier's thought has been a powerful incentive to the Co-operative Movement and its labours, in particular to the Consumer Co-operatives; but the constructive thinking of "utopian socialism" has only been able to accept him by transcending his ideas.

Fourier's *chef d'œuvre* appeared in 1822, the *Traité d'Association Domestique Agricole*; Saint-Simon's *Le Système Industriel* in

1821 and 1822; and from 1820 dates Robert Owen's *Report to the County of Lanark*, which appeared in 1821 and was the matured presentation of his "plan". But Fourier's *La Théorie des Quatre Mouvements et des Destinées Générales*, which contains his system in a nutshell, had already appeared in 1808; Saint-Simon's *De la Réorganisation de la Société Européenne* in 1814; Owen's *A New View of Society*—the theoretical foundation of his plans—in 1813 and 1814. If we go still further back in time we come to Saint-Simon's earliest work at the turn of the century, in which the impending crisis of humanity is already announced, and Fourier's article on universal harmony, which may be regarded as the first sketch of his doctrine. At the same time, however, we find Owen engaged in purely practical activity as the leader of the cotton-spinners in New Lanark, in which capacity he brought about some exemplary social innovations. Unlike that of Saint-Simon and Fourier his doctrine proceeds from practice, from experiment and experience. No matter whether he knew of Fourier's theories or not, Owen's teaching is, historically and philosophically speaking, a rejoinder to theirs, the empirical solution of the problem as opposed to the speculative one. The social units on which society is to be built anew can in this case be called organic; they are numerically limited communities based on agriculture and sustained by the "principle of united labour, expenditure and property, and equal privileges", and in which all members are to have "mutual and common interests". Already we see how Owen, as distinct from Fourier, presses forward to the simple pre-requisites for a genuine community where the rule is not necessarily and exclusively common ownership, but rather a binding together and "communizing" of property; not equality of expenditure, but rather equality of rights and opportunities. "Communal life," says Tönnies of the historical forms of "community", i.e. the "true and enduring forms of men's life together", is "*mutual* possession and enjoyment, and possession and enjoyment of *common* property". In other words, it is a common housekeeping in which personal possessions can stand side by side with common ones, save that through the building of a common economy (quite otherwise than in the scheme of Fourier) only a narrow margin is set between differences in personal possessions and that, as a result of mutuality, of mutual give and take, there arises that very condition which is here termed "mutual possession and enjoyment", i.e. the appropriate participation of all members in one another. Precisely this conception underlies Owen's plan. (Later he goes further and reckons common ownership and co-operative union among the basal foundations of his projected Colony.) He does not fail to appreciate that great educational activity is required for its realization. "Men have not yet been trained in principles that will permit them to act in union, except to defend themselves or to destroy others.... A necessity, however, equally powerful, will now compel men to be trained to act together to create and conserve." Owen knew that ultimately it was a matter of transforming the whole social order, and in particular the relationship between the rulers and the ruled. "The interest of those who govern has ever appeared to be, and under the present systems ever will appear to be, opposed to the interest of those whom they govern." This must continue "while man remains individualized", that is, while society refuses to build itself up out of the real bonds between individuals. The change will reach completion in each single one of the village communities planned, before it extends from them to the community as a whole. The Committee governing the individual village will "form a permanent, experienced local government, never opposed to, but always in closest union with, each individual governed". Certainly there remain at the outset the problems of what Owen calls "the connection of the new establishments with the Government of the country and with the old society", but from his appellation "the old society" it is clear that Owen is thinking of the new society as growing out of the old and renewing it from within. At the same time various stages in the evolution of the new society will have of necessity to exist side by side. A characteristic example of this is given in the Draft of Statutes (inspired by Owen) put forward by the "Association of All Classes of All Nations", founded in 1835, which, using a term that had only just begun to be current in this sense, called itself "The Socialists". Of the three divisions of this association the lower two have only the function of Consumer Co-operatives; the third and highest, on the contrary, is to establish a brotherhood and sisterhood which shall form a single class of producers and consumers differentiated by age alone, "without priests, lawyers, soldiery, buyers and sellers". This is Utopia, to be sure, but a Utopia of that special kind without which no amount of "science" can transform society.

The line of development leading from Saint-Simon to Fourier and Owen rests on no sequence in time; the three men whom Engels names as the founders of socialism worked in approximately the same period; one could almost say that it is a development in contemporaneity. Saint-Simon lays down that society should progress from the dual to the unitary, the leadership of the whole should proceed from the social functions themselves, without the political order superimposing itself as an essentially distinct and special class. To this Fourier and Owen reply that this is only possible and permissible in a society based on joint production and consumption, i.e. a society composed of units in which the two are conjoined, hence of smaller communities aiming at a large measure of self-sufficiency. Fourier's answer affirms that each of these units is to be constituted like the present society in respect of property and the claims of the individual, only that the resultant society will be led from contradiction to harmony by the concord of instinct and activity. Owen's answer, on the other hand, affirms that the transformation of society must be accomplished in its total structure as well as in each of its cells: only a just ordering of the individual units can establish a just order in the totality. This is the foundation of socialism.

IV

PROUDHON

"WHEN the contradictions of '*communauté*' and democracy," Proudhon wrote in a letter of 1844, "once revealed, have shared the fate of the Utopias of Saint-Simon and Fourier, then socialism, rising to the level of a science—this socialism which is neither more nor less than political economy—will seize hold of society and drive it with irresistible force towards its next destination. . . . Socialism has not yet attained to self-consciousness; to-day it calls itself communism." The first sentence reminds one in many respects of the later formulations of Marx. Three months before the letter was written Marx had met Proudhon, who was ten years his senior, in Paris, immediately to conduct night-long conversations with him.

Little as Proudhon wished to go back to the "utopian" systems and deeply as he was opposed to their principles, he nevertheless continued the line of development that began with them. He continued this line by drawing it afresh, only on a higher plane where everything anterior to it was taken for granted. All the same he had a profound fear of himself adding a new system to the old. "System," he wrote in 1849, "I have no system, I will have none and I expressly repudiate the suggestion. The system of humanity, whatever it be, will only be known when humanity is at an end. . . . My business is to find out the way humanity is going and, if I can, prepare it." The real Proudhon is very far removed from the man Marx attacks in his polemic and earlier in a letter to a Russian friend, from the man for whom, as the letter says, "categories and abstractions are the primary facts", "the motive forces which make history" and which it is sufficient to alter for alterations to follow in real life. This "hegelizing" of Proudhon misfires. No man has questioned more honestly and more pungently than Proudhon the social reality of his time and sought its secret. "The economic categories," declared Marx in his polemic, "are only theoretical expressions for the social relationships of production," whereas Proudhon, he says, saw in these relationships only the embodiments of principles; but the fixed social relationships are produced by human beings just as are cloth, linen, etc. Proudhon rightly remarks in the margin of his copy of the polemic: "That is exactly what I'm saying. Society creates the laws and the raw material of its experience." In one of his later, and most mature, writings— *Du Principe Fédératif* (1863)—he pronounces the same judgment from another angle, when he says of reason that it leads the movement of history towards freedom but only on condition that it takes the nature of the forces concerned into account and respects their laws.

Proudhon's fear of "systems" has its roots in his fundamental relationship to social reality. He observes society in all its contrasts and contradictions and will not rest until he has understood and expressed them. Proudhon was a man who had the strength and courage to steep himself in contradiction and bear the strain of it. He did not remain in it in quite the way that Unamuno thinks, who compares him in this respect to Pascal; he did, however, remain in it for so long as was necessary for him to grasp it in all its cruelty, to resolve "the conflict of elements, the clash of contrasts" fully in his thought. And sometimes it was *too* long, judged by the shortness of human life. When Unamuno says of Pascal that his logic was not dialectics but polemics, this is true also of Proudhon to a certain extent; but when he goes on to say that Pascal did not seek any synthesis between thesis and antithesis, it is not in reality true of Proudhon. He sought no synthesis in the Hegelian sense, no negation of negation; he sought, as he says in a letter of 1844, "des resolutions synthétiques de toutes les contradictions", and what he actually means is that he was seeking the way, the way out of contradiction recognized in all its pitilessness, out of the social "antinomies" (as he says, transferring the term from Kant's theory of cognition to the sphere of sociology). For him, thesis and antithesis were categories not embodying themselves in different historical epochs, but coexisting; he took over only the formalism of Hegel, but of Hegel the historian almost nothing. Despite his excursions into history Proudhon was not an historical thinker; his thought was social-critical, and that was both his strength and his limitation. To grasp the contradiction which could, in any given social

reality, in fact be grasped was, for him, the intellectual pre-
requisite for the discovery of "the way". That is why he puts
tendencies and counter-tendencies side by side and refuses to
elevate either of them into an Absolute. "All ideas," he writes
in the *Philosophy of Progress* (1851), "are false, i.e. contradictory
and irrational, when you grant them an exclusive and absolute
meaning, or when you let yourself be swept away by this
meaning"; all tendencies towards exclusiveness, towards
immobility, tend towards degeneration. And just as no
spiritual factors may be regarded as reigning with absolute
necessity, neither may material ones be so regarded. Proudhon
believes neither in blind providence from below, which contrives the salvation of mankind out of technical and material
changes, nor in a free-ranging human intellect, which contrives
systems of absolute validity and enjoins them on mankind.
He sees humanity's real way in the deliverance from false
faiths in absolutism, from the dominion of fatality. "Man no
longer wishes to be mechanized. He strives towards 'defataliza-
tion'." Hence the "universal antipathy to all Utopias whose
essence is political organization and a social credo", by which
Proudhon—in 1858—means Owen, Fourier and the Saint-
Simonist Enfantin, and also Auguste Comte.

Proudhon teaches that no historical principle can be adequately summed up in any system of ideas; every such principle
needs interpretation and may be interpreted well or ill, and the
interpretations influence, directly or indirectly, the historical
fate of the principle. It must, however, be noted as an additional complication that in no age is any one principle all-
powerful. "All principles," writes Proudhon in his posthumous
work *Cæsarism and Christianity*, "are contemporaneous in
history as they are in reason." It is only that they have different
strengths in relation to one another at different epochs. At a
time when a principle is struggling for hegemony it is important
that it should enter man's consciousness and work on his will
in its true essence and not in a distorted form. The "social age"
announced with the French Revolution—an age preceded at
the outset, naturally, by a period of transition, the "era of
Constitutions", just as the Augustan epoch preceded the
Christian: both of them working a renewal, but not a renewal
that goes to the heart of existence—this social age is
characterized by the predominance of the economic principle
over those of religion and government. This principle it is

that "in the name of socialism is stirring up a new revolution in Europe which, once it has brought about a federative Republic of all the civilized states, will organize the unity and solidarity of the human species over the whole face of the earth". It is important to-day to understand the economic principle in its true nature so as to guard against fatal conflicts between it and a travesty of it which usurps its ideas.

As I have said Proudhon did not merely continue the evolutionary line of "utopian" socialism, he began it again from the beginning, but in such a way that everything anterior to him appeared completely remodelled. More especially he did not set out at the point where Saint-Simon stopped; rather he posed Saint-Simon's demand for an economy based on and conditioned by its groupings, in an altogether new and more comprehensive way that goes much deeper into social reality. Saint-Simon started from the reform of the State, Proudhon from the transformation of society. A genuine reconstruction of society can only begin with a radical alteration of the relationship between the social and the political order. It can no longer be a matter of substituting one political régime for another, but of the emergence, in place of a political régime grafted upon society, of a régime expressive of society itself. "The prime cause of all the disorders that visit society," says Proudhon, "of the oppression of the citizens and the decay of nations, lies in the single and hierarchical centralization of authority. . . . We need to make an end of this monstrous parasitism as soon as possible." We are not told why and since when this need has become so pressing, but we can easily remedy this when we realize two things. First: so long as society was richly structured, so long as it was built up of manifold communities and communal units, all strong in vitality, the State was a wall narrowing one's outlook and restricting one's steps, but within this wall a spontaneous communal life could flourish and grow. But to the extent that the structure grew impoverished the wall became a prison. Second: such a structurally poor society awoke to self-consciousness, to consciousness of its existence as a society in contrast to the State, at the time of the French Revolution, and now it can only expect a structural renewal by limiting all not-social organizations to those functions which cannot be accomplished by society itself, —while on the other hand the proper management of affairs grows out of the functioning society and creates its own organs. "The limitation of the State's task is a matter of life and death for freedom, both collective and individual." It is obvious that Proudhon's basic thought is not individualistic. What he opposes to the State is not the individual as such but the individual in organic connection with his group, the group being a voluntary association of individuals. "Since the Reformation and especially since the French Revolution a new spirit has dawned on the world. Freedom has opposed itself to the State, and since the idea of freedom has become universal people have realized that it is not a concern of the individual merely, but rather that it must exist in the group also." In the early writings of Proudhon a sort of individualism still predominates, but already he knows that "through monopoly mankind has taken possession of the globe, and through association it will become its real master". In the course of development, however, individualism beat an increasingly rapid retreat (despite the toleration of individual peasant property) before an attitude in which the problematical relationship between personality and totality was balanced by the largely autonomous group—the local community or commune—living on the strength of its own interior relationships. Although the structural point of view as such is never expressly stated in Proudhon we notice that he comes nearer and nearer to it: his anti-centralism turns more and more to "communalism" and federalism (which indeed, as he says in a letter of 1863, had been boiling in his veins for thirty years), that is, it becomes increasingly structural. Advanced centralization should, he writes in 1860, vanish "once it is replaced by federal institutions and communal customs". What is remarkable here is the connection between the new arrangements to be created—the "institutions", and the community-forms to be retained—the "customs".

Just how powerfully Proudhon felt the amorphous character of present-day society we may learn best, perhaps, from his attitude to the question of universal suffrage. "Universal suffrage," he says in his essay *The Solution of the Social Problem* (1848), "is a kind of atomism by means of which the legislator, seeing that he cannot let the people speak in their essential oneness, invites the citizens to express their opinions per head, *viritim*, just as the Epicurean philosopher explained thought, will and understanding by combinations of atoms." As Proudhon said in his speech to the National Assembly in

1848, universal suffrage needs an "organizing principle". This principle can only rest on the organization of society in groups. "The retention of natural groups," writes Proudhon in 1863, "is of the greatest importance for the exercise of electoral power; it is the essential condition of the vote. Without it there is no originality, no frankness, no clear and unequivocal meaning in the voices. . . . The destruction of natural groups in elections would mean the moral destruction of nationality itself, the negation of the thought of the Revolution." The amorphous basis of elections "aims at nothing less than to abolish political life in towns, communes and departments, and through this destruction of all municipal and regional autonomy to arrest the development of universal suffrage". In such circumstances the body of the nation is but an agglomeration of molecules, "a heap of dust animated from without by a subordinating, centralist idea. In our search for unity, unity itself has been sacrificed". Only as an expression of associated groups will universal suffrage, which is now "the strangling of public conscience, the suicide of the people's sovereignty", become an intelligent, moral and revolutionary force. Provided, of course, that "the various spheres of service are balanced and privilege abolished".

Proudhon by no means fails to recognize that "the real problem to be solved for federalism is not political, but economic". "In order to make the confederation indestructible," he says, "economic right must be declared the foundation of federative right and of all political order." The reform of economic right must follow from the answer to two questions which the workers' Societies have to face: whether labour can be self-financing as regards its undertakings as capital is now, and whether the ownership and control of the undertakings can be collective. "The whole future of the workers," writes Proudhon in a curious book, *The Stockjobber's Handbook* (1853), "depends on the answer to these questions. If the answer is in the affirmative a new world will open out before humanity; if in the negative, then let the proletariat take warning! Let them commend themselves to God and the Church—there is no hope for them this side of the grave." Proudhon's sketch of the affirmative answer is "Mutualism" in its mature form. "Mutuality, reciprocity exists," he writes, "when all the workers in an industry, instead of working for an *entrepreneur* who pays them and keeps their products, work for

one another and thus collaborate in the making of a common
product whose profits they share amongst themselves. Extend
the principle of reciprocity as uniting the work of every group,
to the Workers' Societies as units, and you have created a form
of civilization which from all points of view—political, economic
and æsthetic—is radically different from all earlier civiliza-
tions." This is Proudhon's solution to the problem, and he
formulates it as follows: "All associated and all free." But in
order that this may be so the association must not become a
system imposed from above; rather must people associate in
Workers' Societies (in the sense of "foci of production") only
in so far as—Proudhon writes in 1864—"the demands of production, the cheapness of the product, the needs of consumption and the security of the producers themselves require it".
By associating in this manner the workers are only following
"la raison des choses" itself, and consequently they "can pre-
serve their freedom in the very heart of the society". Thinking
like this it was inevitable that Proudhon should turn in 1848
against the State-financed "social workshops" demanded by
Louis Blanc (as later by Lassalle). He sees in them only a new
form of centralization. It would mean, he says, a number of
large associations "in which labour would be regimented and
ultimately enslaved through a State policy of brotherhood,
just as it is on the point of being enslaved now through the
State policy of capitalism. What would freedom, universal
happiness, civilization have gained? Nothing. We would merely have exchanged our chains and the social idea would have
made no step forward; we would still be under the same
arbitrary power, not to say under the same economic fatalism".
Here Proudhon is expressing the view which we find twenty
years later in theoretical form in Gierke's great work. "Only
free association," says Gierke, "can create communities in
which economic freedom persists. For those organisms which
spring from individual initiative and from the creative powers
of their members enhance the life of each individual member
simultaneously with the newly established life of the whole."
    Communist centralism thus appeared to Proudhon as a
variant of absolutism elaborated to a monstrous and ruthless
degree of perfection. This "dictatorial, authoritarian, doctrinaire system starts from the axiom that the individual is
subordinate, in the very nature of things, to the collectivity;
from it alone does right and life come to him; the citizen belongs

to the State as the child to his family, he is in its power and possession, and he owes it submission and obedience in all things". Just as we can understand from this standpoint that Marx (in a passage intended for the polemic but not actually incorporated in it) said of Proudhon that he was "incapable of comprehending the revolutionary movement", so it is from this standpoint also that we can understand why Proudhon, in an entry in his diary, described Marx as "the tapeworm of socialism". In the communist system common ownership is to bring about the end of all property, personal as well as parochial and communal; universal association is to absorb all special associations, and collective freedom is to devour all corporative, regional and private freedoms. Proudhon defines the political system of centralist communism, in 1864, in words which are worth pondering: "A compact democracy having the appearance of being founded on the dictatorship of the masses, but in which the masses have no more power than is necessary to ensure a general serfdom in accordance with the following precepts and principles borrowed from the old absolutism: indivisibility of public power, all-consuming centralization, systematic destruction of all individual, corporative and regional thought (regarded as disruptive), inquisitorial police." Proudhon thinks that we are not far removed from pure centralist communism in politics and economics, but he is persuaded that "after a final crisis and at the summons of new principles a movement will begin in the reverse direction".

The book in which these words occur—*The Political Capacity of the Working Classes*—was completed only shortly before Proudhon's death. He attributed especial importance to it as setting forth the "idea of a new democracy" and wrote it, as he says, under the inspiration of the "Manifesto of the Sixty"— the electoral declaration (1861) of a group of workers whose ideas for the most part came very near to Proudhon's own. This manifesto was the fourth in the series of four socialist "Manifestos"; the first being the *Manifeste des Égaux* of Babeuf, the second that of the Fourierist Considérant, the third the "Communist Manifesto"—and it was the first to emerge from the proletariat itself. In his declaration, in which Proudhon hails the "awakening of socialism" in France and the "unveiling of corporate consciousness" in the working-class, he demands *inter alia* the setting up of a *chambre syndicale*, but not one which, as some people had proposed in a "strange confusion of thought" (here Saint-Simon's idea turns up again), was to be composed of workers and work-givers; "what we demand is a Chamber composed exclusively of workers elected by the free vote of all—a Chamber of Labour". This demand bears clear witness of the development of the new social thinking from Saint-Simon to Proudhon.

By advancing from the idea of social reconstruction to the idea of structural renewal, Proudhon took the decisive step. The "industrial constitution" of Saint-Simon does not signify a new structure, but "federalism" does.

Proudhon naturally distinguishes two modes of structure, which interpenetrate: the economic structure as a federation of work-groups, which he calls "agrarian-industrial federation", and the political structure, which rests on the decentralization of power, the division of authority, the guarantee of the maximum degree of autonomy to the communes and regional associations, and the widest possible replacement of bureaucracy by a looser and more direct control of affairs arising from the natural group. Proudhon's "Constitutional Science" can be summed up in three propositions. It is necessary—

1. To form moderately sized and moderately autonomous groups and to unite them by an act of federation;
2. To organize the government in each federated State according to the law of the division of organs. That is to say: inside the Public Authority to divide everything that can be divided, to define everything that can be defined, to allocate among different organs and functionaries everything that has been so divided and defined, to leave nothing undivided, and to surround the Public Authority with all the conditions of publicity and control;
3. Instead of allowing the federated States or the provincial and municipal authorities to merge into a central authority, to limit the competence of the latter to the simple tasks of general initiative, mutual assurance and supervision.

The life of a society finds fulfilment in the combination of persons into groups, of groups into associations. "Just as a number of people by their common exertions give rise to a collective strength which is superior in quality and intensity to the sum of their respective strengths, so a number of work-groups associated in a relationship of mutual exchange will generate a potency of a higher order," which can be regarded specifically as "the social potential". Mutualism—the building up of an economy on reciprocity of service, and federation—the building up of a political order on the brotherhood of groups— are only two aspects of the same structure. "Through the grouping of individual strengths and the interdependence of the groups the whole nation will become a body." And a real brotherhood of man can be constituted from the various peoples, as a federation of federations.

Proudhon treated the problem of decentralization more particularly in his *Theory of Taxation* (1861). He says that he is not unaware of the fact that political centralization offers many advantages, but it is too costly. People regard it as obvious not merely because it flatters their collective vanity but also because "in nations as in children reason seeks unity in all things, simplicity, uniformity, identity and hierarchy as well as size and mass", and this is why centralization—the type of all the ancient kingdoms—became an effective method of discipline. "People like simple ideas and are right to like them. Unfortunately the simplicity they seek is only to be found in elementary things; and the world, society and man are made up of insoluble problems, contrary principles and conflicting forces. Organism means complication, and multiplicity means contradiction, opposition, independence. The centralist system is all very well as regards size, simplicity and construction; it lacks but one thing—the individual no longer belongs to himself in such a system, he cannot feel his worth, his life, and no account is taken of him at all." But the conception of and demand for a public system in which the individual can belong to himself, feel his worth and his life, a system that takes account of him as an individual, does not just float about in the boundless realm of abstraction—it is bound to the facts and tendencies of our social reality. In the modern constitutional State "the various groups need no direction in a great many of their activities; they are quite capable of governing themselves with no other inspiration than conscience and reason". In any State organized in accordance with the principles of modern law there occurs a progressive diminution of directive action—a decentralization. And a corresponding development can be discerned on the economic side. The development of technics in our age (Proudhon had already drawn attention to this in 1855 in his book on the reform of the railways, but it was only long after his death, with the mechanization of communications and the prospective electrification of production, that the matter became topical) tends to make the concentration of population in the big cities unnecessary; "the dispersion of the masses and their redistribution is beginning". The political centre of gravity must gradually shift from the cities to "the new agricultural and industrial groupings".

But Proudhon is by no means of the opinion that the process of decentralization is prospering and maturing in all fields. On the contrary: in the field of politics he sees in the conscious will of man a counter-movement of the gravest import. "A fever of centralization," he writes in 1861, "is sweeping over the world; one would say that men were weary of the vestiges of freedom that yet remain to them and were only longing to be rid of them. . . . Is it the need for authority that is everywhere making itself felt, a disgust with independence, or only an incapacity for self-government?" Only the creative, restructuring powers that reign in the depths of man can avail against this "fever", this grave sickness of the human spirit. The expression of these powers is "the idea" of which Proudhon says at the end of a political treatise in 1863 that it "exists and is in circulation", but that, if it is to be realized, it must "issue from the bowels of the situation".

At that time, when his insight was at its height, Proudhon was far from assuming that this situation was imminent. We know from some of his letters of 1860 how he pictured the immediate future. "We should no longer deceive ourselves," he wrote. "Europe is sick of thought and order; it is entering into the era of brute force and contempt of principles." And in the same letter: "Then the great war of the six great powers will begin." A few months later: "Carnage will come and the enfeeblement that will follow these blood-baths will be terrible. We shall not live to see the work of the new age, we shall fight in the darkness; we must prepare ourselves to endure this life without too much sadness, by doing our duty. Let us help one another, call to one another in the gloom, and practise justice wherever opportunity offers." And finally: "To-day civilization is in the grip of a crisis for which one can only find a single analogy in history—that is the crisis which brought the coming · of Christianity. All the traditions are worn out, all the creeds abolished; but the new programme is not yet *ready*, by which I mean that it has not yet entered the consciousness of the masses. Hence what I call *the dissolution*. This is the cruellest moment in the life of societies. . . . I am under no illusions and do not expect to wake up one morning to see the resurrection of freedom in our country, as if by a stroke of magic. . . . No, no; decay, and decay for a period whose end I cannot fix and which will last for not less than one or two generations—is our lot. . . . I shall witness the evil only, I shall die in the midst of the darkness." But the thing is "to do our duty". In the same year he had written to the historian Michelet: "It will only be possible to escape by a complete revolution in our ideas and our hearts. We are working for the revolution, you and I; that will be our honour before posterity, if they remember us." And eight years previously he had replied thus to a friend who had suggested emigration to America: "It is here, I tell you, here under the sabre of Napoleon, under the rod of the Jesuits and the spy-glass of the secret service, that we have to work for the emancipation of mankind. There is no sky more propitious for us, no earth more fruitful."

Like Saint-Simon, though in far greater detail and with far more precision, Proudhon brought the problem of a structural renewal of society to the fore without treating it as such. And just as Saint-Simon failed to face the question of the social units which would serve as the cells of a new society, so Proudhon left it open in all essentials, though he came much closer to it. But in the first case there were contemporaries, and in the second followers, who made this very problem the principal object of their research and planning.

That Proudhon did not study it more intensively has its chief reason in his suspicions of "association" as a State-prescribed uniform panacea for all the ills of society, in the sense proposed by Louis Blanc: "social workshops" in industry as well as in agriculture, established, financed and controlled by the State. It must be noted that Louis Blanc's proposals—if not in intention, at least in character—are socially structural; from the "solidarity of all workers in the same shop" he goes on to the "solidarity of shops in the same industry" and thence to the "solidarity of different industries". Also, he sees the agricultural commune as being built up on the basis of combined production and consumption. "To meet the needs of all," he says in his *Organization of Labour* (1839), "it is necessary to pool the products of the work of all," this is the form in which he sees the immediate possibility of a "more radical and more complete" application of "the system of fraternal association". Proudhon's suspicions were directed, as said, against a new "raison d'État"; hence, against uniformity, against exclusiveness, against compulsion. The co-operative form seemed to him more applicable to industry than to agriculture, where he was concerned for the preservation of the peasantry (note that in all the permutations of his thinking he holds fast to one principle in this connection, that the land lawfully belongs to him who cultivates it) and, when applied to industry, only in those branches whose nature the co-operative form suited, and for certain definite functions. He refuses to equate a new ordering of society with uniformity; order means, for him, the just ordering of multiformity. Eduard Bernstein is quite right when he says that Proudhon denied to the essentially monopolist Co-operative what he conceded to the mutualist one. Proudhon had a profound fear of everything coming "from above", everything imposed on the people and decked out with privileges. In this connection he feared the proliferation of new collective egoisms, for these seemed to him more perilous than individual egoisms. He saw the danger that threatens every Producer Co-operative working for a free market: that it will be seized with the spirit of capitalism, the ruthless exploitation of opportunities and eventualities. His doubts were cogent. They were rooted in his basic view which made justice the criterion of true socialism. (According to him there are two ideas: freedom, and unity or order, and "one must make up one's mind to live with both of them by seeking a balance between them". The principle that permits this is called "justice".) But the structural form of the coming society announced by Proudhon, the form in which the balance of freedom and order is attained and which he calls federalism, required him not merely to concern himself—as he did—with the larger units to be federated (that is, the various nations, but the smaller ones also whose federative combination would in reality alone constitute the "nation". Proudhon did not fulfil this requirement. He could only have fulfilled it had he sought in it and from it the answer to his own doubts, which is to say, only if he had directed his best thought to the problem of how to promote and organize "association" in such a way that the danger inherent in it would be, if not exorcized, at least appreciably diminished. Because he did not do this sufficiently well—important as was the step taken in this direction by his principle of mutualism—we find here no adequate answer to our question: "What are the units which will federate in a new and genuine popular order?", or, more precisely: "How must the units be constituted so that they can federate into a genuine popular order, a new and just social structure?" Thus Proudhon's socialism lacks one essential. For we cannot but doubt whether existing social units, even where the old community-forms remain, can still, being what they are, combine in justice; also whether any new units will ever be capable of it unless this same combination of freedom and order governs and shapes their inception.

V

KROPOTKIN

THIS is where Kropotkin comes in. Born at a time—a hundred years ago—when Proudhon was just beginning his struggle against the inequity of private property, against property as "theft", he consciously takes up Proudhon's legacy so as to amplify and elaborate it. At the same time he simplifies it, though often in a fruitful and stimulating way. He simplifies Proudhon by mitigating the dazzle of contradictory principles, and that is something of a loss; but he also translates him into the language of history, and that is a gain. Kropotkin is no historian; even where he thought historically he is a social geographer, a chronicler of the states and conditions on earth; but he thinks in terms of history.

Kropotkin simplifies Proudhon first of all by setting up in the place of the manifold "social antinomies" the simple antithesis between the principles of the struggle for existence and mutual help. He undertakes to prove this antithesis biologically, ethnologically and historically. Historically he sees these principles (probably influenced very strongly by Kireyewski's picture of historical duality in 1852) crystallizing on the one hand into the coercive State, on the other into the manifold forms of association such as the County Commune, the parish, the guild, the corporation and so on right up to the modern Co-operatives. In an over-elaborate and historically under-substantiated formulation written in 1894, Kropotkin puts the antithesis thus: "The State is an historical growth that slowly and gradually, at certain epochs in the life and history of all peoples, displaces the free confederations of tribes, communities, tribal groups, villages and producers' guilds and gives minorities terrible support in enslaving the masses—and this historical growth and all that derives from it is the thing we are fighting against." Later (in his book *Modern Science and Anarchy*, a complete French edition of which appeared in 1913) he found a more correct and historically a more justifiable formulation. "All through the history of our civilization," he writes, "two contrary traditions, two trends have faced one another: the Roman tradition and the national tradition; the imperial and the federal; the authoritarian and the libertarian. And once more, on the eve of social revolution, we find these two traditions face to face." Here, probably under the influence of Gierke, who called the two opposing principles domination and free association, there is a hint, bound up with Kropotkin's historical insight, that the universal conflict of the two spiritual forces persists inside the social movement itself: between the centralist and the federalist forms of socialism.

Certainly Kropotkin's conception of the State is too narrow; it is not a question of identifying the centralist State with the State in general. In history there is not merely the State as a clamp that strangles the individuality of small associations; there is also the State as a framework within which they may consolidate; not merely the "great Leviathan" whose authority, according to Hobbes, is based on "terror", but also the great nourishing mother who carefully folds her children, the communities, to her bosom; not merely the *machina machinarum* that turns everything belonging to it into the components of some mechanism, but also the *communitas communitatum*, the union of the communities into community, within which "the proper and autonomous common life of all the members" can unfold. On the other hand, Kropotkin was more or less right when he dated the inception of the modern centralist State—which he confused with the State as such—from the sixteenth century; from the time when "the downfall of the free cities" was sealed "by the abolition of all forms of free contract": the village communities, the Societies of Artisans, the fraternities, the confederacies of the Middle Ages. "With some certainty we may say," writes the legal historian Maitland, "that at the end of the Middle Ages a great change in men's thought about groups of men was taking place." Now "the Absolute State faces the Absolute Individual". In Gierke's words "the sovereign State and the sovereign individual fought to define their natural and lawful spheres of existence; all intermediate associations were degraded to merely legalistic and more or less arbitrary formations and at last completely exterminated". In the end nothing remained but the sovereign State which, in proportion to its mechanization, devoured everything living. Nothing organic could resist "the rigidly centralized directive mechanism which, with its enormous expenditure of human intelligence, could be operated at the touch of a button", as Carl Schmitt, the ingenious interpreter of totalitarianism, calls the Leviathan. Those for whom the important thing is not so much the security of individuals (for which purpose the Leviathan is deemed indispensable) as the preservation of the substance of community, the renewal of communal life in the life of mankind— are bound to fight against every doctrine that would defend centralism. "There is no more dangerous superstition," says the church historian Figgis, "than that political atomism which denies all power to societies as such, but ascribes absolutely unlimited competence over body, soul and spirit to the grandiose unity of the State. It is indeed 'the great Leviathan made up of little men' as in Hobbes' title-page, but we can see no reason to worship the golden image." In so far as Kropotkin did battle not with State-order itself but with the centralist State-apparatus, he has powerful allies in the field of science. In scientific circles it may perhaps be maintained against "pluralism" that the modern State, in so far as it is pluralist rather than totalitarian, has the appearance of a "compromise between social and economic power-groups, an agglomeration of heterogeneous factors, parties, interests, concerns, trades-unions, churches, etc." (Carl Schmitt.) But that says nothing against a socialistic rebuilding of the State as a community of communities, provided that the communities are real communities; for then all the various groups Schmitt mentions would either not exist or be quite different from what they are now, and the fusion of the groups would not be an agglomeration but, in Landauer's words, "a league of leagues". Any element of compulsive order still persisting would only represent the stage of development attained by man at the time; it would no longer represent the exploitation of human immaturity and human contrasts. Contrasts between individuals and between groups will probably never cease, nor indeed should they; they have to be endured; but we can and we must strive towards a state of things where individual conflicts neither extend to large wholes which are not really implicated, nor lend themselves to the establishment of absolute centralist suzerainty.

As in his inadequate distinction between the excessive and the legitimate State, or the superfluous and the necessary State, so in another important respect Kropotkin's view, although perceiving many historical relationships unnoticed by Proudhon, is not realistic enough. He says on one occasion that in his (Kropotkin's) praise of the medieval commune he might perhaps be accused of having forgotten its internal conflicts, but that he had by no means done so. For history showed that "these conflicts were themselves the guarantee of free life in the free city", that the communities grew and were rejuvenated through them. Further, that in contrast to the wars of States, these inter-communal conflicts were concerned with the struggle for and maintenance of the individual's freedom, with the federative principle, the right to unite and to act in unison, and that therefore "the epochs when the conflict was fought out in freedom without the weight of existing authority being thrown into either of the scales, were the epochs of greatest spiritual development". This is substantially right and yet one all-important point has not been sufficiently grasped. The danger of collective egoism, as also that of schism and oppression, is hardly less in an autonomous community than in the nation or party, particularly when the community participates as a co-partner in production. A telling example of this is to be found in the internal development of the "mining communities", that is, the Producer Co-operatives of mine-workers in the German Middle Ages. Max Weber has shown in a scholarly exposition that in the first stage of this there was an increasing expropriation of the owners; that the community became the managing director and shared out the profits while observing as far as practicable the principle of equality; but that a differentiation among the workers themselves thereupon set in. For as a result of increasing demand the new arrivals were no longer accepted into the community, they were "non-union men", hired labour, and the process of disintegration thus initiated continued until purely capitalist "interested parties" permeated the personnel of the mining-community and the union finally became a capitalistic instrument which itself appointed the workers. When we read to-day (for instance in Tawney's book *The Acquisitive Society*) how the workers can "freeze out" the owners from industrial undertakings by making them superfluous through their own control of production; or how they can limit the interest of the owners to such an extent that the latter become mere *rentiers* with no share in the profits and no responsibility—precisely, therefore, what had happened in the German mines seven hundred years ago—then the historical warning comes very close to us and commands us to have a care, to build the checks on collective egoism into the new order of society. Kropotkin is not blind to this danger; for instance, he points out (*Mutual Aid*, 1902) that the modern Co-operative Movement which, originally and in essence, had the character of mutual aid, has often degenerated into "share-capital individualism" and fosters "co-operative egoism".

Kropotkin realized very clearly that, as Proudhon had already indicated, a socialistic community could only be built on the basis of a double intercommunal bond, namely the federation of regional communes and trade communes variously intercrossing and supporting one another. To this he sometimes added as a third principle, communal groupings based on voluntary membership. He sketches a picture of the new society most vividly in his autobiography (1899), in that passage where he speaks of the basic views of the anarchist-communist "Jura-Federation" founded by Bakunin, in which he played an active part in 1877 and in the years immediately following. From the documents of the Jura-Federation itself no comparable formulation is indeed known to us, and it is to be assumed that Bakunin's ideas, which were never other than cursorily sketched, becoming in the course of years intertwined with those of Proudhon, only attained maturity in Kropotkin's own mind. "We remark in the civilized nations," he writes in his autobiography, "the germ of a new social form which will supplant the old. . . . This society will be composed of a number of societies banded together for everything that demands a common effort: federations of producers for all kinds of production, of Societies for consumption; federations of such Societies alone and federations of Societies and production groups, finally more extensive groups embracing a whole country or even several countries and composed of persons who will work in common for the satisfaction of those economic, spiritual and artistic needs which are not limited to a definite territory. All these groups will unite their efforts through mutual agreement. . . . Personal initiative will be encouraged and every tendency to uniformity and centralization combated. Moreover this society will not ossify into fixed and immovable forms, it will transform itself incessantly, for it will be a living organism continually in development." No equalization, no final fixation—that is Kropotkin's basic idea, and it is a healthy one. What is aspired to is, as he says in 1896, "the fullest development of individuality combined with the highest development of free association in all its aspects, in all possible degrees and for all conceivable purposes: an ever-changing association bearing in itself the elements of its own duration and taking on the forms which at any moment best correspond to the manifold endeavours of all." And he adds with emphasis in 1913: "We conceive the structure of society to be something that is never finally constituted."

Such a structure means mobilizing the social and political spontaneity of the nation to the greatest possible degree. This order, which Kropotkin calls Communism (a term usurped by that "negation of all freedom" so bitterly attacked by Proudhon) and which may be called more correctly Federal Communalism, "cannot be imposed—it could not live unless the constant, daily collaboration of all supported it. In an atmosphere of officialdom it would suffocate. Consequently it cannot subsist unless it creates permanent contacts between everybody for the thousand and one common concerns; it cannot live unless it creates regional and autonomous life in the smallest of its units—the street, the house-block, the district, the parish." Socialism "will have to find its own form of political relationships. . . . In one way or another it will be more 'of the people'; will have to be closer to the *forum* than parliamentary government is. It will have to depend less on representation, more on self-government". We see particularly clearly here that Kropotkin is ultimately attacking not State-order as such but only the existing order in all its forms; that his "anarchy", like Proudhon's, is in reality "anocracy" ($\dot{\alpha}\kappa\rho\alpha\tau\dot{\iota}\alpha$); not absence of government but absence of domination. "If I may express myself so," Proudhon had written in a letter of 1864, "anarchy is a form of government or constitution in which the principle of authority, police institutions, restrictive and repressive measures, bureaucracy, taxation, etc., are reduced to their simplest terms." This is at bottom Kropotkin's opinion too. As the important words "*less* representation" and "*more* self-government" show, he also knows that when it comes to our real will for a "restructuring" of society, it is not a question of manipulating an abstract principle but only of the *direction* of realization willed; of the limits of realization possible in this direction in any given circumstances—the line that defines what is demanded here and now, becomes attainable.

He knows that tremendous things are willed and how deeply they reach into our hearts: "All the relations between individuals and between the masses have to be corrected"; but he also knows that this can only be done if social spontaneity is roused and shown the direction in which it has to work.

That a decisive transformation of the social order as a whole cannot ensue without revolution is self-evident for Kropotkin. So it was for Proudhon. In the book that Marx attacked as "petty bourgeois" Proudhon knew well enough that the mighty task he set the working-classes—namely to "bring forth from the bowels of the people, from the depths of labour a greater authority, a mightier fact, which will draw capital and the State into its orbit and subdue them"—cannot be fulfilled without revolution. Proudhon saw in revolutions, as he said in a toast to the Revolution of 1848, "the successive declarations of human justice", and the modern State he held to be "counter-revolutionary in nature and in principle". What he contested (in his famous letter to Marx) was that "no reform was possible at present without a *coup de main*" and that "we were obliged to use revolutionary action as a means of social reform". But he divined the tragedy of revolutions and came to feel it more and more deeply in the course of disappointing experiences. Their tragedy is that as regards their *positive* goal they will always result in the exact opposite of what the most honest and passionate revolutionaries strive for, unless and until this has so far taken shape *before* the revolution that the revolutionary act has only to wrest the space for it in which it can develop unimpeded. Two years before his death Proudhon remarks bitterly: "It is the revolutionary struggle that has given us centralization." This view was not unfamiliar to Kropotkin. But he believed that it was sufficient to influence the revolutionary force by education so as to prevent the revolution from ending in a new centralization "every bit as bad or worse", and thus enabling "the people—the peasants and the urban workers—to begin the really constructive work themselves". "The point for us is to *inaugurate* the social revolution through communism." Like Bakunin, Kropotkin misses the all-important fact that, in the social as opposed to the political sphere, revolution is not so much a creative as a delivering force whose function is to set free and authenticate—i.e. that it can only perfect, set free, and lend the stamp of authority to something that has already been foreshadowed in the womb of the pre-revolutionary society; that, as regards social evolution, the hour of revolution is not an hour of begetting but an hour of birth—provided there was a begetting beforehand.

Of course there are in Kropotkin's teaching fundamental elements which point to the significance of pre-revolutionary structure-making. As in his book on mutual aid he traces the vestiges of old community-forms in our society and compares them with examples of existing, more or less amorphous solidarity, so in his book *Fields, Factories and Workshops* (1898, enlarged edition 1912) he makes, on purely economic and industrial-psychological grounds, a weighty contribution to the picture of a new social unit fitted to serve as a cell for the formation of a new society in the midst of the old. As against the progressive over-straining of the principles of division of labour and excessive specialization, he sets the principle of labour-integration and the alliance of intensive agriculture with decentralized industry. He sketches the picture of a village based on field and factory alike, where *the same* people work in the one as in the other alternately without this in any way entailing a technological regress, rather in close association with technical developments and yet in such a way that man enters into his rights as a human being. Kropotkin knows that such an alteration cannot be "completely carried through" in a society like ours, nevertheless he plans not merely for to-morrow but for to-day as well. He stresses the fact that "every socialistic attempt to alter the present relations between capital and labour will come to grief if it disregards the trend towards integration"; but he also stresses that the future he wishes to see "is already possible, already realizable". From there it is only a step to demanding that an immediate beginning be made with the restructuring of society—but that step is decisive.

VI

LANDAUER

LANDAUER'S step beyond Kropotkin consists primarily in his direct insight into the nature of the State. The State is not, as Kropotkin thinks, an institution which can be destroyed by a revolution. "The State is a condition, a certain relationship between human beings, a mode of human behaviour; we destroy it by contracting other relationships, by behaving differently." Men stand to one another to-day in a "statual" relationship, that is, in one which makes the coercive order of the State necessary and is represented by it and in it. Hence this order can only be overcome to the extent that this relationship between men is replaced by another. This other relationship Landauer calls "People". "It is a connexion between people which is actually there; only it has not yet become bond and binding, is not yet a higher organism." To the extent that people, on the basis of the processes of production and circulation, find themselves coming together again as a People and "growing together into an organism with countless organs and members", Socialism, which now lives only in the minds and desires of single, atomized people, will become reality—not in the State "but outside, without the State", and that means *alongside* the State. This "finding themselves together" of people does not, as he says, mean the founding of something new but the actualization and reconstitution of something that has always been present—of Community, which in fact exists alongside the State, albeit buried and laid waste. "One day it will be realized that socialism is not the invention of anything new but the discovery of something actually present, of something that has grown." This being so, the realization of socialism is always possible if a sufficient number of people want it. The realization depends not on the technological state of things, although socialism when realized will of course look differently, begin differently and develop differently according to the state of technics; it depends on people and their spirit. "Socialism is possible and impossible at all times; it is possible when the right people are there to will and do it; it is impossible when people either don't will it or only supposedly will it, but are not capable of doing it."

From this glimpse into the real relationship between State and Community some important things ensue. We see that, practically speaking, it is not a question of the abstract alternative "State or No-State". The Either-Or principle applies primarily to the moments of genuine decision by a person or a group; then, everything intermediate, everything that interposes itself, is impure and unpurifying; it works confusion, obscurity, obstruction. But this same principle becomes an obstruction in its turn if, at any given stage in the execution of the decision reached, it does not permit *less* than the Absolute to take shape and so devalues the measures that are *now* possible. If the State is a relationship which can only be destroyed by entering into another relationship, then we shall always be helping to destroy it to the extent that we do in fact enter into another.

To grasp the subject fully we must go one step further. As Landauer pointed out later, "State" is status—a state, in fact. People living together at a given time and in a given space are only to a certain degree capable, of their own free will, of living together rightly; of their own free will maintaining a right order and conducting their common concerns accordingly. The line which at any time limits this capacity forms the basis of the State at that time; in other words, the degree of incapacity for a voluntary right order determines the degree of legitimate compulsion. Nevertheless the *de facto* extent of the State always exceeds more or less—and mostly very much exceeds—the sort of State that would emerge from the degree of legitimate compulsion. This constant difference (which results in what I call "the excessive State") between the State in principle and the State in fact is explained by the historical circumstance that accumulated power does not abdicate except under necessity. It resists any adaptation to the increasing capacity for voluntary order so long as this increase fails to exert sufficiently vigorous pressure on the power accumulated. The "principial" foundations of the power may have crumbled, but power itself does not crumble unless driven to it. Thus the dead can rule the living. "We see," says Landauer, "how something dead to our spirit can exercise living power over our body." The task that thus emerges for the socialists, i.e. for all those intent on a restructuring of society, is to drive the factual base-line of the State back to the "principial" base-line of socialism. But this is precisely what will result from the creation and renewal of a real organic structure, from the union of persons and families into various communities and of communities into associations. It is this growth and nothing else that "destroys" the State by displacing it. The part so displaced, of course, will only be that portion of the State which is superfluous and without foundation at the time; any action that went beyond this would be illegitimate and bound to miscarry because, as soon as it had exceeded its limits it would lack the constructive spirit necessary for further advance. Here we come up against the same problem that Proudhon had discovered from another angle: association without sufficient and sufficiently vital communal spirit does not set Community up in the place of State—it bears the State in its own self and it cannot result in anything but State, i.e. power-politics and expansionism supported by bureaucracy.

But what is also important is that for Landauer the setting up of society "outside" and "alongside" the State is essentially "a discovery of something actually present, something that has grown". In reality a community does exist alongside the State, "not a sum of isolated individual atoms but an organic cohesion that only wants to expand and, out of many groups, form a great arch". But the reality of community must be roused, must be summoned out of the depths where it lies buried under the incrustations of the State. This can only happen if the hard crust that has formed on mankind, if their own inner "statehood" is broken open and the slumbering, immemorial reality aroused beneath. "Such is the task of the socialists and of the movements they have started among the peoples: to loosen the hardening of hearts so that what lies buried may rise to the surface: so that what truly lives yet now seems dead may emerge and grow into the light." Men who are renewed in this way can renew society, and since they know from experience that there is an immemorial stock of community that has declared itself in them as something new, they will build into the new structure everything that is left of true community-form. "It would be madness," Landauer writes in a letter to a woman who wanted to abolish marriage, "to dream of abolishing the few forms of union that remain to us! We need *form*, not formlessness. We need *tradition*." He who builds, not arbitrarily and fruitlessly, but legitimately and for the future, acts from inner kinship with age-old tradition, and this entrusts itself to him and gives him strength. It will now become clear why Landauer calls the "other" relationship which men can enter into instead of the ordinary State-relationship, not by any new name but simply "People". Such a "People" comprehends also the innermost reality of "Nationhood"—what remains over when "Statehood" and politicization have been superseded: a community of being and a being in manifold community. "This likeness, this equality in inequality, this peculiar quality that binds people together, this common spirit, is an actual fact. Do not overlook it, you free men and socialists; socialism, freedom and justice can only be accomplished between those who have always been united; socialism cannot be established in the abstract, but only in a concrete multiplicity that is one with the harmony of the peoples." The true connexion between Nation and socialism is discovered here: the closeness of people to one another in mode of life, language, tradition, memories of a common fate—all this predisposes to communal living, and only by building up such a life can the peoples of the earth constitute themselves anew. "Nothing but the rebirth of all peoples out of the spirit of regional community can bring salvation." And Landauer understands "regional community" quite concretely, in the reappearance—if only in a rudimentary state—of the traditional community-forms and in the possibility of preserving them, renewing and expanding them. "The radical reformer will find nothing to reform, now or at any other time, except what is there. Hence, now and at all times it is well for the regional community to have its own boundaries; for part of it to be communal land, for the other parts to be family property for house, yard, garden and field." Landauer is counting here on the long memories of communal units. "There is so much to which we could add whatever outward forms of life still contain living spirit. There are village communities with vestiges of ancient communal property, with peasants and labourers who remember the original boundaries that have been in private possession for centuries; communal institutions embracing agricultural work and the handicrafts." To be a socialist means to be livingly related to the life and spirit of the community; to keep on the alert; to examine with impartial eye whatever vestiges of this spirit yet lurk in the depths of our uncommunal age; and, wherever possible, to bind the newly created forms firmly to the forms that endure. But it also means: to guard against all rigid delineation of ways and methods: to know that in the life of man and human communities the straight line between two points is often the longest; to understand that the real way to socialist reality is revealed not merely in what "I know" and what "I plan", but also in the unknown and unknowable; in the unexpected and the not to be expected; and, so far as we can, to live and act accordingly at all times. "We know absolutely no details," says Landauer in 1907, "about our immediate way; it may lead over Russia, it may lead over India. The only thing we know is that our way does not lead through the movements and struggles of the day, but over things unknown, deeply buried, and sudden."

Landauer said once of Walt Whitman, the poet of heroic democracy whom he translated, that, like Proudhon (with whom in Landauer's opinion he had many spiritual affinities), Whitman united the conservative and the revolutionary spirit— Individualism and Socialism. This can be said of Landauer too. What he has in mind is ultimately a revolutionary conservation: a revolutionary selection of those elements worthy to be conserved and fit for the renovation of the social being.

Only on these assumptions can we understand Landauer as a revolutionary. He was a man from south-western Germany, of the Jewish middle class, but he came much nearer to the proletariat and the proletarian way of life than Marx, also a south-west German of the Jewish middle class. Again and again Marxists have condemned his proposals for a socialist Colony as implying a withdrawal from the world of human exploitation and the ruthless battle against it, to an island where one could passively observe all these tremendous happenings. No reproach has ever been falser. Everything that Landauer thought and planned, said and wrote—even when it had Shakespeare for subject or German mysticism, and especially all designs whatsoever for the building of a socialistic reality—was steeped in a great belief in revolution and the will for it. "Do we want to retreat into happiness?" he wrote in a letter (1911). "Do we want our lives for ourselves? Do we not rather want to do everything possible for the people, and long for the impossible? Do we not want the whole thing—Revolution?" But that long-drawn struggle for freedom which he calls Revolution can only bear fruit when "we are seized by the spirit, not of revolution, but of regeneration"; and the individual revolutions taking place within that long "Revolution" seem to Landauer like a fire-bath of the spirit, just as in the last analysis revolution is itself regeneration. "In the fire, the ecstasy, the brotherliness of these militant movements" says Landauer in his book *The Revolution*, which he wrote in 1907, at my request, "there rises up again and again the image and feeling of positive union through the binding quality, through love—which is power; and without this passing and surpassing regeneration we cannot go on living and must perish." It is important, however, to recognize without illusion that "although Utopia is prodigally beautiful—not so much in *what* it says as in *how* it says it—the end which revolution actually attains is not so very different from what went before". The strength of revolution lies in rebellion and negation; it cannot solve social problems by political means. "When a revolution," Landauer continues, speaking of the French Revolution, "ultimately gets into the terrible situation that this one did, with enemies all round it inside and out, then the forces of negation and destruction that still live on are bound to turn inwards and against themselves; fanaticism and passion turn to distrust and soon to blood-thirstiness, or at least to an indifference to the added terrors of killing; and before long terror by killing becomes the sole possible means for the rulers of the day to keep themselves pro-visionally in power." Thus it happened (as Landauer, his view unchanged, wrote ten years later about the same revolution) that "the most fervent representatives of the revolution thought and believed in their finest hours—no matter to what strange shores they were ultimately flung by the raging waves—that they were leading mankind to a rebirth; but somehow this birth miscarried and they got in each other's way and blamed each other because the revolution had allied itself to war, to violence, to dictatorship and authoritarian oppression—in a word, to politics". Between these two statements Landauer, writing in July, 1914, on the threshold of the first World War, expressed the same critical insight in a particularly topical form. "Let us be under no illusion," he says, "as to the situation in all countries to-day. When it comes to the point, the only thing that these revolutionary agitations have served is the nationalist-capitalist aggrandisement we call imperialism; even when originally tinctured with socialism they were all too easily led by some Napoleon or Cavour or Bismarck into the mainstream of politics, because all these insurrections were in fact only a means of political revolution or nationalist war but could never be a means of socialist transformation, for the sufficient reason that the socialists are romantics who always and inevitably make use of the means of their enemies and neither practise nor know the means of bringing the new People and the new humanity to birth." But already in 1907 Landauer, basing himself on Proudhon, had drawn the obvious conclusion from his views. "It will be recognized sooner or later that, as the greatest of all socialists—Proudhon—has declared in incomparable words, albeit forgotten to-day, social revolution bears no resemblance at all to political revolution; that although it cannot come alive and remain living without a good deal of the latter it is nevertheless a peaceful structure, an organizing *of* new spirit *for* new spirit and nothing else." And further: "Yet it is the case, as Gottfried Keller says, that the last triumph of freedom will be dry. Political revolution will clear the ground, literally and in every sense of the word[1]; but at the same time those institutions will be preparing in which the confederation of industrial societies can live, the confederation destined to release the spirit that lies captive behind the State." This preparation, however, the real "transformation of society, can only come in love, in work and in stillness". Hence it is obvious that the spirit that is to be "released" must already be alive in people to an extent sufficient for such "preparation", so that they may prepare the institutions and the revolution as "clearing the ground" for them. Once again Landauer refers to Proudhon. In the revolutionary epoch of 1848 Proudhon had told the revolutionaries: "You revolutionaries, if you do *that* you will make a change indeed." Disappointed, he had other things to do afterwards than repeat the catchwords of the revolution. "Everything comes in time," says Landauer, "and every time after the revolution is a time before the revolution for all those whose lives have not got bogged in some great moment of the past." Proudhon went on living, although he bled from more than one wound; he now asked himself: " '*If* you do that,' I said—but *why* have you not done it?" He found the answer and laid it down in all his later works, the answer which

---

[1] "Den Boden frei machen" also means to "free the land", make it available to the people. The phrase is used in this latter sense in the next paragraph. Trans.

in our language runs: "Because the spirit was not in you."

Again, we are indebted to Landauer rather than to Kropotkin for one vital clarification. If political revolution is to serve social revolution three things are necessary. Firstly: the revolutionaries must be firmly resolved to clear the ground and make the land available[1] as communal property, and thereafter to develop it into a confederation of societies. Secondly: communal property must be so prepared in institutions as to ensure that it can be developed along those lines after the ground has been cleared. Thirdly: such preparations must be conducted in a true spirit of community.

The significance of this third item, the "spirit", for the new society-to-be is something that none of the earlier socialists recognized as profoundly as did Landauer. We must realize what he means by it—always assuming of course that we do not understand spiritual reality merely as the product and reflection of the material world, as mere "consciousness" determined by the social "being" and explicable in terms of economic-technical relationships. It is rather an entity *sui generis* that stands in close relation to the social being, without, however, being explicable at any point in terms of the latter.

"A degree of high culture is reached," says Landauer, "when the various social structures, in themselves exclusive and independent of one another, are all filled with a uniform spirit not inherent in or proceeding from these structures, but reigning over them purely in its own right. In other words: such a degree of culture arises when the unity pervading the various forms of organization and the supra-individual formations is not the external bond of force, but a spirit dwelling in the individuals themselves and pointing beyond earthly and material interests." As an example Landauer cites the Christian Middle Ages (truly the sole epoch in the history of the West comparable in this respect with the great cultures of the Orient). He sees the Middle Ages as characterized not by this or that form of social life, such as the County Commune, the guilds, corporations and trade-confraternities, the city-leagues, nor even by the feudal system, the churches and monasteries and chivalric orders—but by this "totality of independent units which all interpenetrate" to form "a society of societies". What united all the variously differentiated forms and "bound

[1] See footnote, p. 52.

them together at the apex into a higher unity, a pyramid whose point was not power and not invisible in the clouds, was the spirit streaming out of the characters and spirits of individual men and women into all these structures, drawing strength from them and streaming back into the people again". How can we invoke this spirit in a time like ours, "a time of unspirituality and therefore of violence; unspirituality and therefore mighty tension within the spirits of individuals; individualism and therefore atomization, the masses uprooted and drifting like dust; a time without spirit and therefore without truth?" It is "a time of decay, and therefore of transition". But because this *is* so, in such a time and only in such a time will the spirit be conjured to reappear; such conjurations are the revolutions. What, however, makes room for the spirit is the attempt at realization. "Just as the County Communes and numerous other instruments of stratification and unification were there *before* the spirit filled them and made them what they have meant to Christendom; and just as a kind of walking is there before the legs develop, and just as this walking builds and fashions the legs—so it will not be the spirit that sends us on our way, but our way that will bring the spirit to birth in us." But this road leads "those who have perceived how impossible it is to go on living as they are, to join together and put their labour at the service of their needs. In settlements, in Societies—despite all privation". The spirit that animates such people helps them along their common way, and on this way and on it alone can it change into the new spirit of community. "We socialists want to give spirit the character of reality so that, as unitive spirit, it may bring mankind together. We socialists want to render the spirit sensible and corporeal, we want to enable it to do its work, and by these very means we shall spiritualize the senses and our earthly life." But for this to happen the flame of the spirit must be carefully tended in the settlements lest it go out. Only by virtue of living spirit are they a form of realization; without it they become a delusion. "But if the spirit lives in them it may breathe out into the world and suffuse all the seats of co-operation and association which, without it, are but empty shells, gaols rather than goals. We want to bring the Co-operatives, which are socialist form without socialist content, and the trades-unions, which are valour without avail—to Socialism, to great experiments." "Socialism," says Landauer in 1915, "is the attempt to lead man's common life to a bond of common spirit in freedom, that is, to religion." That is probably the only passage where Landauer, who always eschewed all religious symbolism and all open avowals of religion, uses the word "religion" in this positive and binding sense—uses it to express the thing he craves: a bond of common spirit in freedom.

This state of affairs should not wait on our expectations; it should be "attempted" and a beginning be made. In his striving for "common spirit" Landauer knows that there is no room for this without the land, i.e. that it can only have room to the extent that the soil once more supports man's communal life and work. "The struggle of socialism is the struggle for the soil." However, if the great upheaval is to occur in the "conditions of soil-ownership " (as it is called in the twelve Articles of the Socialist League founded by Landauer), "the workers must first create, on the basis of their common spirit—which is the capital of socialism—as much socialist reality, and exemplify it, as is possible at any time in proportion to their numbers and their energy." Here a beginning *can* be made. "Nothing can prevent the united consumers from working for themselves with the aid of mutual credit, from building factories, workshops, houses for themselves, from acquiring land; nothing—if only they have a will and begin." Such is the vision of the community, the archetype of the new society, that floats before Landauer's eyes; the vision of the socialist village. "A socialist village, with workshops and village factories," says Landauer in 1909, continuing Kropotkin's thought, "with fields and meadows and gardens, with livestock large and small, and poultry—you proletarians of the big cities, accustom yourselves to this thought, strange and odd as it may seem at first, for that is the only beginning of true socialism, the only one that is left us." On these seemingly small beginnings (on whether they arise or not), depends the revolution and whether it will find something worth fighting for—something which the hour of revolution itself is unable to create. But whether it finds this something and secures its full development, on this depends in its turn whether socialist fruit will ripen on revolutionary fields apart from the usual political crop.

Although, therefore, there is no beginning, no seed for the future other than what people now living under the rule of capitalism can achieve in their life together, in a common life based on common production and consumption, despite all the weariness, misery and disappointment—yet Landauer is far from regarding these results as the final form of realization. Like Proudhon and Kropotkin he, too, has little faith in hitching the demands of socialism to the dreams, visions, plans and deliberations of men living to-day. He knows well enough "the strange circumstance that this precarious beginning, this 'Socialism of the Few'—the settlement—bears many resemblances to the hard and toilsome communism of a primitive economy". Nevertheless the "essential thing" for him is "to accept this communist-looking state not as an ideal but as a necessity for the sake of socialism, as a first stage—because we are the beginners". From there the road will lead "as quickly as may be" to a society, in outlining which Landauer blends the ideas of Proudhon and Kropotkin: "a society of equalitarian exchange based on regional communities, rural communities which combine agriculture with industry." But even here Landauer does not see the absolute goal, only the immediate objective "so far as we can see into the future". All true socialism is relative. "Communism goes in search of the Absolute and can naturally find no beginning but that of the word. For the only absolute things, detached from all reality, are words."

Socialism can never be anything absolute. It is the continual becoming of human community in mankind, adapted and proportioned to whatever can be willed and done in the conditions given. Rigidity threatens all realization, what lives and glows to-day may be crusted over to-morrow and, become all-powerful, suppress the strivings of the day after. "Everywhere, wherever culture and freedom are to dwell in unison, the various bonds of order must complement one another, and the fixity of the whole must bear in itself the principle of dissolution. . . . In an age of true culture the order of private property, for instance, will bear in itself, as a revolutionary, dissolvent and re-ordering principle, the institution of *seisachtheia*[1] or Year of the Jubilee." True socialism watches over the forces of renewal. "No final security measures should be taken to establish the millennium or eternity, but only a great balancing of forces, and the resolve periodically to renew the

---

[1] A "shaking off of burdens", the name given to the "disburdening ordinance" of Solon, by which all debts were lowered. Trans.

balance. . . . 'Then may you cause trumpets to be blown throughout the land!' The voice of the spirit is the trumpet. . . . Revolt for constitution; reform and revolution the one rule valid for all time; order through the spirit the one intention— these were the great and holy things in the Mosaic order of society. We need them again, we need redirection and convulsion through the spirit, which has no desire to fix things and institutions in their final forms, but only to declare itself everlastingly. Revolution must become the accessory of our social order, the corner-stone of our constitution."

VII

EXPERIMENTS

WITH the same over-simplification that labelled the early
socialists "utopian", people called the two great waves of the
Co-operative Movement that agitated the bulk of the working
population of England and France in 1830 and 1848,
"romantic"—and with no greater justification in so far as this
word implies dreaminess and unreality of outlook. These
waves were no less expressions of the deep-seated crises accom-
panying the mechanization of modern economy than were the
political movements proper—Chartism in England and the two
Revolutions in France. But, as distinct from the latter, which
wanted to alter the whole hierarchy of power, the Co-operative
Movements wanted to begin with the creation of social reality,
without which no amount of tinkering with legal relationships
can ever lead to socialism. They have been accused of rating
man's share in the desired transformation too high and the
share of circumstance too low; but there is no way of taking the
measure of man's potentialities in a given situation that has to
be changed, except by demanding the extraordinary. The
"heroic" forms of the Co-operative Movement credited their
members with a loyalty and readiness for sacrifice which, in
the long run at any rate, they were unable to meet; but that
does not prove in the least that loyalty and readiness for
sacrifice, present though they may be in exceptional periods of
political upheaval, cannot be found to a sufficient degree in the
daily round of economic life. It is easy to scoff and say that the
initiators of the heroic Co-operative Movements "put the ideal
man in the place of the real one"; but the "real" man
approximates most closely to the "ideal" just when he is
expected to fulfil tasks which he is not up to, or thinks he is
not up to—not of the individual alone is it true that "he grows
to his higher purposes". And finally, it depends on the goal,
the consciousness of it and will for it. The heroic epoch of the

modern Co-operative looked to the transformation of society, the epoch of technics looks essentially to the economic success of each individual co-operative undertaking. The first has come to grief, but that does not condemn the goal and the way towards it; the second has great successes to record, but they do not look at all like stages on the way to the goal. A champion of the bureaucratized co-operative system expresses himself thus on its origin: "Let us give our fullest admiration to those humble and faithful souls who were guided by the burning torch of social conviction. . . . But let us acknowledge that heroism is not in itself a condition of soul fitted to bring about economic results." True enough; but let us also acknowledge that economic results are not in themselves fitted to bring about a restructuring of human society.

As regards the three chief forms of co-operation (apart from the Credit Co-operatives), to wit, Consumer Co-operatives, Producer Co-operatives, and Full Co-operatives[1] based on the union of production and consumption—let us compare a few dates taken from the two epochs of this movement.

The 1830 epoch: 1827 saw the first English Consumer Co-operative in the modern sense founded under the influence of the ideas of Dr. William King; 1832 the first French Producer Co-operative set up according to the plans of Buchez; in between the experimental "settlements" of Owen and his adherents—the American experiment and the English ones.

The 1848 epoch: first the Consumer Co-operative of the Rochdale weavers, then Louis Blanc's "national workshops" and the like, finally, by way of travesty, the tragi-comic "Icaria" project of Cabet (who was a *real* Utopian in the negative sense, a social constructionist without the slightest understanding of human fundamentals) on the banks of the Mississippi. Of these no more will be said here—as attempts to realize "utopian" Socialism—than is deemed desirable for the purpose of this book.

King and Buchez were both doctors and both, in contrast to Owen—whose war against religion was one of the main tasks of his life—practising Christians, one Protestant, one Catholic. This is not without significance. For Owen socialism was the fruit of reason, for King and Buchez it was the realization of the teachings of Christianity in the domain of public

---

[1] *Vollgenossenschaft* is evidently a term coined by the author. It is here translated literally since no equivalent term is to be found in the English authorities. Trans,

life. Both held, as Buchez says, that the moment had come
"to mould the teachings of Christianity into social institutions".
This basic religious feeling profoundly influenced the whole
outlook of the two men; with King, who was in sympathy with
the Quakers and worked together with them, it influenced the
very tone of his words—everywhere we feel an unabstract,
immediate, upwelling concern for his fellow-men, their life
and soul.

King has justly been called in our own day—once he was
rescued from oblivion—the first and greatest of the English
theoreticians of the Co-operative Movement. But over and
above this he had the gift of the simple word, which made
plain to everybody the essential nature of the things he spoke of.
In the whole literature of the Co-operatives I know nothing
that gives such an impression of the "popular" and the
"classical" alike as do the twenty-eight numbers of the magazine
called *The Co-operator*, which King wrote and brought out
between 1828 and 1830 for the instruction of those who were
actively spreading his ideas. He had a depth and clarity of
social perception like none of his contemporaries, with the
exception of the more scientific, but also more abstract,
William Thompson. He starts from work as "the root of the
tree, to whatever size it may ultimately grow". Work is "in
this sense everything". The working classes "have the
monopoly of this article". No power on earth can rob them
of it, for all power is "nothing more than the power to direct
the labour of the working classes". What they lack is capital,
that is, disposal of the machines and the possibility of maintaining themselves whilst working them. But "all capital is made
out of labour", and it is "nothing in itself". It has to unite
with labour in order to be productive. This union is now
achieved by capital "buying and selling the labourer like
a brute". True union, "the natural alliance", can only be
brought about by the working-classes themselves, only they
do not know it. Their sole hope of achieving it is to get together,
co-operate, make common capital, become independent. King
gives passionate expression to the thought already uttered by
Thompson before him, of co-operation as the form of production peculiar to labour. "As soon as ever the labourers unite
upon a labour principle instead of a capital principle, they will
make the dust fly in all directions . . . and it is great odds but
this dust will blind some of the masters." If the workers get

together they can acquire the tools they need—the machines—and themselves become, in their Co-operatives, the subject of production. But they can also acquire the land. King says clearly that he sees only a beginning in the Consumer Co-operatives, that his goal, like Thompson's, is the Full Co-operative. As soon as they can dispose of sufficient capital the "Society", that is, the Co-operative Society, "may purchase land, live upon it, cultivate it themselves and produce any manufactures they please, and so provide for all their wants of food, clothing, and houses. The Society will then be called a Community." King calls upon the trades-unions to purchase land with their savings and settle their unemployed members on it in communities producing above all for their own needs. These communities will embrace not merely the specific interests and functions of their members but their life as well, in so far as they want and are able to live it in common. But the life-community, even if it can only come to full reality in the Full Co-operative, should already exist potentially in the relations of the members of the Consumer Co-operative to one another. King is thinking not of a bare impersonal solidarity but of a personal relationship, generally latent yet ready at any time to become actual, a "sympathy that would act with new energies, and rise occasionally even to enthusiasm". Hence only members capable of such a relation are admitted. The basic law of co-operative means, for King, the establishment of genuine relations between man and man. "When a man enters a Co-operative Society, he enters upon a new relation with his fellow men; and that relation immediately becomes the subject of every sanction, both moral and religious." It is obvious that this ideal, this "heroic" demand could not be upheld in succeeding years, when membership of the Co-operatives increased with their growing mechanization and bureaucratization; but seen from the standpoint of social re-structure, this is the cause of the inadequacy of these "partial" Co-operatives.

When William King suspended publication of *The Co-operator* in 1830, three hundred Societies had come into being under the influence of his teachings. These for the most part did not live long because of the "spirit of selfishness" reigning in them. as one of the leaders told the Congress of 1832. The crucial stage of the consumer-based Co-operatives did not begin until 1844, when in the grave industrial crisis which had once again descended upon England shortly after the collapse of a strike, a little group of flannel-weavers and representatives of other trades met in the city of Rochdale to ask one another: "What can we do to save ourselves from misery?" There were not a few among them who thought that each man must begin with himself—and indeed that is always right in all circumstances, for without it nothing can ever succeed; only one must know that it is merely a part of what has to be done, albeit an important part. And because they did not know this they proposed to renounce the pleasures of alcohol, and they naturally failed to convince their comrades. (How important none the less the proposal seemed can be seen from the fact that subsequently, in the Statutes of the "Equitable Pioneers of Rochdale", the erection of a Temperance Hotel was mentioned on the agenda of the Society.) And again there were some, members of the Chartist Movement which aimed at altering the Constitution and seizing power, who proposed that they should ally themselves to political action so as to win for Labour its due share in legislation; but the movement had passed its peak and they had learned that although the political struggle was necessary it was not enough. Some of Owen's adherents who were among those assembled declared that there was no hope for them in England any more and that they must emigrate and build a new life for themselves abroad (thinking perhaps of the possibility of new experimental Settlements in America); but that too was rejected, for the predominant feeling was: "doing" means doing *here*, means not fleeing before the crisis but enduring it with what strength one has. This strength was little enough, yet a few of the weavers who were fairly familiar with the teachings of William King pointed out that they could put their strengths together and then perhaps a power would be there with which they could *do* something. So they decided to "co-operate".

The tasks the Society set itself were put very high, without the authors of the statutes being accused of overbold imagination. These tasks were ranged in three stages. The first, the Consumer Co-operative, was regarded as something to be organized at once. The second, the Producer Co-operative, comprising the common building of houses for the members, the common production of wares and the common cultivation of allotments by unemployed comrades, was likewise a prospect for a not far distant future, though not the immediate future.

The third stage, the Co-operative Settlement, was removed still further by the proviso "as soon as practicable": "as soon as practicable this Society shall proceed to arrange the powers of production, distribution, education, and government; or, in other words, to establish a self-supporting Home Colony of united interests or assist other Societies in establishing such Colonies." It is amazing how the practical intuition of the flannel-weavers of Rochdale grasped the three essential fields of co-operation. In the first field, the Consumer Co-operative, their simple and effective methods (among which the distribution of profits among members according to the relative volume of purchases proved to be particularly persuasive) blazed a new trail. In the field of production they made a number of advances with increasing success, particularly in corn-milling but also in the field of spinning and weaving; yet it is characteristic of the whole problem (to be discussed later) of co-operative activity in production that, in the steam spinning-mills constructed by the Equitable Pioneers, only about half the workers were members of the Society, and hence stockholders, and that these immediately put through the principle of rewarding work with payment but of distributing the profit exclusively among the stockholders as "*entrepreneurs* and owners of the business", as the important co-operationist Victor Aimé Huber, who repeatedly visited Rochdale in its early days, remarks in his monograph on the Pioneers. They did not, however, get down to the third, the greatest and decisive task, of realizing the Co-operative Colony based on joint production and consumption.

One element in the Rochdale institution deserves our particular attention. That is the co-operation between the Co-operatives, the working together of several co-operative groups and institutes, which was undertaken by the "Pioneers" themselves and, later, in conjunction with them. "The principle of Federalism," says the Rumanian scholar Mladenatz in his *History of the Co-operative Theories,* obviously basing himself on Proudhon, "derives quite naturally from the idea itself, which is the foundation of the co-operative system. Just as the Co-operative Society unites people for the common satisfaction of certain needs, so the various co-operative cells unite one with another by applying the principle of solidarity for the common exercise of certain functions, particularly those of production and supply." Here we again meet the arch-principle of restructuring, although naturally the consumer associations as such, i.e. Co-operatives which only combine certain interests of people but not the lives of the people themselves, do not appear suited to serve as cells of a new structure.

The modern Consumer Co-operative which has become so great a reality in the economic life of our time derives from the ideas of "utopian" socialism. In William King's plans there is a clearly discernible tendency to reach the great socialist reality through the creation of small socialist realities which keep on expanding and confederating continually. But King recognized at the same time, and with the utmost clarity, the nature of the technological revolution that had started in his day. He recognized the cardinal significance of the machine and approved it; he rejected all assaults on machines as "folly and criminality". But he also recognized that the inventors, who are workers too, destroy themselves and their comrades with their "wonderful inventions", because "by selling these inventions to their masters they work *against* themselves, instead of keeping them in their own hands and working *with* them". For this it is necessary, of course, that the workers should constitute themselves co-operatively in their Societies. "The workmen have ingenuity enough to make all the machinery in the world, but they have not yet had ingenuity enough to make it work *for* them. This ingenuity will not be dormant much longer." Consequently co-operative organization of consumption is, for King, only a step towards the co-operative organization of production, but this in its turn is only a step towards the co-operative building of life as a whole.

In the hundred years since its inception the Consumer Co-operative has conquered a considerable portion of the civilized world, but the hopes that King set on its internal development have not yet been fulfilled. Consumer Societies may in many places, and sometimes to a very great extent, have turned to production for their own needs, and there exists, as Fritz Naphtali rightly stresses, a tendency to penetrate more and more deeply into production and guide it in the direction of "basic" production. But we have hardly come any nearer to an organic alliance of production and consumption in a comprehensive communal form, although we already have notable examples of large Consumer Societies—or groups of the same for individual branches of production—organizing themselves into Producer Co-operatives, or assimilating existing

ones; but that is only technical organization, not the fulfilment of genuine co-operative thought. And just as little has
the confederation of local societies, even where this has occurred
on a large scale, preserved a genuine federative character; in
these cases the small Societies have mostly, as was reported
several decades ago, changed from independent foci of social
solidarity into mere organs of membership, and their stores into
mere branches of the organization as a whole. The technological
advantages of such centralization are obvious; the trouble is
that there was no authority at hand to try to salvage as much
autonomy in the individual Societies as was compatible with
technological requirements, although people did try here and
there—for instance in Switzerland—to counteract the progressive "de-souling" and de-substantiation of the Societies by
planned decentralization. But for the most part the running
of large co-operative institutions has become more and more
like the running of capitalist ones, and the bureaucratic
principle has completely ousted, over a very wide field, the
voluntary principle, once prized as the most precious and
indispensable possession of the Co-operative Movement. This is
especially clear in countries where Consumer Societies have in
increasing measure worked together with the State and the
municipalities, and Charles Gide was certainly not far wrong
when he called to mind the fable of the wolf disguised as a
shepherd and voiced the fear that, instead of making the State
"co-operative", we should only succeed in making the Co-
operative "static". For the spirit of solidarity can in truth only
remain alive to the extent that a living relationship obtains
between human beings. Tönnies thought that in their
transition to communal buying and then to producing
for their own needs the Consumer Societies would "lay the
foundations of an economic organization that would stand in
open opposition to the existing social order", and that *in theory*
"the capitalist world would therefore be lifted off its hinges".
But "theory" can never become reality so long as the life-
forms of capitalism permeate co-operative activity.

Buchez, who came shortly after King and who planned and
inspired the founding of Producer Co-operatives in France, is
likewise a "utopian" socialist at bottom. "The Communist
reform that is everywhere in the air," he writes in his magazine
L'Européen in 1831, "should be implemented by the *association*
of workers." For Buchez—who, although a Catholic, graduated

in the school of Saint-Simon where he was in sympathy with the radical socialist Bazard—production is everything and the organization of consumption not even a stage. In his opinion the Producer Co-operative—by which he, with less understanding of technological developments than King, means manual workers rather than modern industrial workers—leads directly to the socialist order. "The workers of a particular trade unite, put their savings together, raise a loan, produce as they think best, repay the borrowed capital despite great privations, ensure that each man gets equal pay, and leave the profits in the common funds, with the result that the co-operative workshop becomes a little industrial community." *Une petite communauté industrielle*—here Buchez comes close to King's idea that a Society can become a Community, save that he prematurely ascribes this character to the Producer Co-operative as such, whereas King's deeper insight envisaged such a possibility only for the Full Co-operative. Buchez concludes with the simple, all too simple, formula: "Let all the workers do this and the social problem will be solved." He knew well enough that the great problem of ownership of the land was not solved by it in the least, so he devised the makeshift slogan: "The land for the peasants, the workshop for the workers" without appreciating the question of the social reform of agriculture in its true import; the problem of evolving a Full Co-operative, the all-important problem of social re-structure, was hidden from him, though not from King. On the other hand Buchez recognized with astounding acuteness most of the dangers that threaten the socialist character of the Producer Co-operative from within, one above all, the increasing differentiation inside the Co-operative in its initial stages between those comrades who have founded it and the workers who come afterwards—a differentiation which lends the Co-operative, though it plead socialism never so energetically, the incontestable stamp of an appendage to the capitalist order. To eliminate this danger Buchez built two counter-measures into the modified programme he published after his first practical experiences of 1831: firstly the "social capital" accruing at any time from the putting by of a fifth of the profits was to remain the inalienable, indivisible property of the Society, which was itself to be declared indissoluble and was to replenish itself continually by taking on new members; and secondly, the Society might not employ outside workers as wage-earners for longer than one year, after which time it was bound to accept new comrades according to its requirements (in a sample contract published in 1840 in the journal of the Buchezites, *L'Atelier*, the term was reduced to a trial period of three months). To the first of these points Buchez says that, but for this capital the Society "would resemble all the other trade societies; it would be useful only to the founders and harmful to all who had taken no part in the beginning, for in the hands of the former it would ultimately become an instrument of exploitation". As has rightly been said, this programme aimed at the creation of a capital which would finally absorb "the industrial capital of the whole country and thus realize the appropriation of all the means of production through Workers' Co-operatives". Here, too, we find that "utopian" element again; but, which is the more practical in the last analysis: to try to create social reality through social reality, with its rights defended and extended by political means, or to try to create by the magic wand of politics alone? Naturally enough the two rules were only followed very irregularly by the Societies founded under Buchez' influence, and after twenty years the principle of indivisible capital was made so questionable that those who remained true to it had to wage a hard and virtually fruitless fight for it, as for the principle whereby the conditions of property would be changed and capital would come under the rule of work—a principle that had to be upheld if the Co-operative was to benefit the whole of the working-class and not merely "the few fortunate founders who, thanks to it, had become *rentiers* instead of wage-earners". And just about this time, 1852, we read of similar experiences in England in a report of the Society for the Promotion of Working-men's Associations. But from all of them, from the analogous experiences in the Middle Ages as also from similar experiences in the history of the Consumer Societies, there is no other conclusion to be drawn save that the internal problems of the Co-operatives and the dominance of the capitalist principle that still persists in them can be overcome, albeit gradually, only in and through the Full Co-operative.

It is likely that Louis Blanc was influenced by Buchez' thought; but he differs from him on decisive points. At the same time the important thing is not that he demanded, as Lassalle did later for his Worker-Producer Co-operatives, State help for the "social workshops" he wanted to found, since "what the proletariat lacks in order to free itself is tools, and it is the government's job to deliver them". That was, of course, a deep-seated error, indeed a contradiction in terms, since a government representative of a definite State-order cannot very well be urged to call institutions into being which are destined (such was Blanc's express meaning) to abolish that order. It was only logical, therefore, that the anti-socialist majority in the Provisional Government of 1848 should first replace Blanc's plan by a caricature and then play havoc even with this; but as regards the nature of the social reform he planned this demand of Blanc's was not absolutely essential. Far more significant is the fact that Blanc's social programme was itself centralist in thought: he wanted each large industry to constitute itself as a single association by grouping itself round a central workshop. He gave this basically Saint-Simonistic thought a federalist tinge by demanding that the solidarity of all the workers in one workshop should be continued in the solidarity of all the workshops in one branch of industry and finally completed in the solidarity of all the branches of industry; but what he called solidarity was in actual fact more like solidification into centralist management with monopoly status. Well might Blanc be anxious to attack "the cowardly and brutal principle" of competition, as he once called it in the National Assembly, at the root; that is, to prevent collective competition from emerging in the place of individual competition. And this is indeed the chief danger, apart from internal differentiation, that threatens the Producer Co-operative. A good example of the widespread incidence of this danger is afforded by a letter written by one of the leaders of the Christian-Socialist Co-operative movement in England at that time, in which he says of the Producer Co-operatives founded by this movement that they were "actuated by a thoroughly mercenary competitive spirit" and "aimed merely at a more successful competition than is possible under the present system". This danger was recognized by Buchez and his adherents; but they refused to combat it with monopolies which seemed to them even more dangerous, because monopoly meant for them the paralysis, the end of all organic development. According to their proposals competition between the Co-operatives was rather to be organized and regulated by means of a league of the Co-operatives themselves. Here free federation opposes planned amalgamation. But we have to acknowledge that the federalist idea crops up again and again with Blanc and bursts the centralist strait-jacket, particularly of course after the failure of his State plan. He gives a twist to Buchez' plan for reserve funds by intending it to "realize the principle of mutual help and solidarity between the various social workshops". But as soon as he proceeds from the plan for State initiative to the planning of free Co-operatives he sees no other way of reaching this goal except the way of federation, beginning with the Co-operatives already existing; these are to come to an understanding with one another and name a Central Committee which shall organize throughout the country "the most important of all subscriptions—the subscription to abolish the proletariat". Such words are midway between the sublime and the ridiculous; but the call to the proletariat for self-abolition through co-operation implies a certain practical seriousness which is not without significance for the time that followed. And towards the end of 1849 we see Blanc expressing his approval of the *Union des associations fraternelles*, which arose out of the federation of more than a hundred Co-operatives and realized his enemy Proudhon's idea of the *mutualité du travail;* backing himself up, of course, by saying that on the agenda of the Union there was talk of "centralizing business-matters of general interest". Everywhere in Blanc we come across thoughts which belong to the living tradition and context of "utopian" socialism. He sees the Producer Co-operative emerging into the Full Co-operative in the future, just as King saw the Consumer Co-operative merging into it; in which respect, just as the *Union des associations fraternelles* praised by him aimed at establishing, *as a federation,* "agricultural and industrial colonies" on a large scale, so he was aiming at the creation of Communal Home Colonies. His starting-point is the technological necessity for large-scale concerns: "We must inaugurate a system of large-scale concerns for agriculture by linking them up with association and common ownership," and he wants if possible to transplant industry to the country and "wed industrial work to agricultural". Here, too, Kropotkin's idea of a "division of labour in time", of the union of agriculture, industry and handicraft in a modern village-community, is anticipated.

Despite the early suppression of the Co-operative Federations by the Reaction, numerous new Producer Co-operatives came into being in France during the following years; even doctors and chemists united on a co-operative basis (in these cases there could obviously be no question of genuine Producer Co-operatives, since there is no place for communal work here). The enthusiasm for Co-operatives outlasted the Revolution. Even the persecution and dissolution of many of the Co-operatives after the *coup d'état* was unable to check the movement. The real danger threatening them here as in England came from within: their capitalization, their gradual transformation into capitalist or semi-capitalist societies. Forty years after the enthusiastic efforts, beginning about 1850, of the English Christian Socialists to create a wide net of Workers' Producer Co-operatives which "rejected any notion of competition with each other as inconsistent with the true form of society", Beatrice Webb stated that with the exception of a few Co-operatives which had remained more or less true to the ideal of a "brotherhood of workers"—most of which, however, had become questionable at one point or another— all the rest "exhibit an amazing variety of aristocratic, plutocratic and monarchical constitutions".   And fifty years after Louis Blanc there was a thoroughly typical (in this respect) Producer Co-operative in France, that of the spectacle-makers, which, apart from a small number of *associés* and approximately as many *adhérents*, employed ten times as many wage-earners. Despite this, however, we can find perfect examples of the inner battle for socialism everywhere. Sometimes there is something tragic about them, but equally something prophetic. The Producer Co-operative has rightly been called "the child of sorrows and the darling" of all those "who expect the Co-operative Movement to produce something essential for the salvation of mankind"; but it is readily understandable from the facts that a champion of the Consumer Co-operative Societies should call the Producer Co-operatives which work for the open market "thoroughly unsocialistic in spirit and in essence", because "producers, set up by and for themselves, always and in all circumstances have separatist, individualist or cliquish interests".   Apart, however, from the exaggeration inherent in such an assertion, Producer Co-operatives above all should never be "set up by and for themselves". Two great principles should together guard against this: the combination of production and consumption in the Full Co-operative, and Federalism.

The development of the Consumer Co-operative follows the

straight line of numerical progression; a considerable portion of civilized mankind (characteristically enough, outside America) is organized to-day, from the consumption side, on co-operative lines. On the other hand the development of the Producer Co-operatives (I speak here only of the Producer Co-operative in the strict sense, not of the many partial, in the main agricultural associations which aim merely at making production easier or more intensive), can be represented as a zig-zag line which, on the whole, shows hardly any upward trend. New ones are always coming into being, but again and again most of the more vigorous ones pass over into the sphere of capitalism; there is hardly any continuity. The Full Co-operative, however, is in different case; its development, so far as there is one, looks like a cluster of small circles between which there is generally no real connexion. Consumer and Producer Co-operatives were based on an extensive movement which spread to locality after locality; Colonies in the Full Co-operative sense have always had something sporadic, improvised, lacking in finality about them. In contrast to the others they also lacked what Franz Oppenheimer has termed "the power of remote effect". Not but what some of them got themselves talked about; but their power of attraction was individualistic, they did not call new community-cells into being. In the history of Co-operative Colonies, neither in Europe (with the exception of Soviet Russia, where, however, the essential basis of free will and autonomy does not exist) nor with few exceptions in America is there any indication of a federative tendency. Consumer Co-operatives have continually and increasingly federated; Producer Co-operatives in the true sense have done so discontinuously, now on the increase, now on the decrease; communal Colonies in general not at all. Their fate is at odds with their will: originally they did not want to become isolated, but they did become isolated; they wanted to become working models, but they only became interesting experiments; they wanted to be the dynamic and dynamitic beginnings of a social transformation, but each had its end in itself. The cause of this difference between the Consumer and Producer Co-operative on the one hand and Full Co-operative on the other seems to me ultimately to lie in an essential difference of starting-point. The former grew out of given situations which were roughly the same in a whole chain of places and factories, so that from the start there was a germ of reciprocal influence in the experiments undertaken to get the situation in hand, and hence the germ of their federation. In addition the plans that inspired the founding of these Co-operatives did not derive from one all-embracing thought, but from a question addressed, as it were, to the planners by the situation itself. We can accurately follow this process with King and Buchez, because both were federalists at the outset; Buchez even had a federative association in mind for the trades-unions he had proposed. In both cases the plans were directed towards remedying a given state of distress, and they bore a local character in so far as they sought to solve the problems of this emergency at the point where these problems brought themselves to bear. Such plans may be called topical in the precise sense of being locative, inasmuch as they were of their own nature related to definite localities, the very ones in which the problems arose. The identity of the problems in different places led at once to the possibility of federative union, right up to gigantic formations like some associations of Consumer Co-operatives to-day.

It is a fundamentally different story with the generality of "colonial" Full Co-operatives. Here, time after time, with greater or lesser independence of the situation but always without real reference to given localities and their demands, we see the "idea" dictating its decrees, preparing its plans somewhere up in the clouds and then bringing them down to earth. No matter how speculative these plans are in origin and therefore thoroughly schematic as with Fourier; no matter how much they are based on definite experiences and empirical assumptions as with Owen, they will never answer the questions put by a given situation, but will proceed to create new situations irrelevant to the locality and its local problems. This becomes peculiarly evident where Settlements in foreign countries are concerned: emigration is not organized and regulated along socialistic lines, no such thing; rather the impulse to emigrate is associated with a new impulse, namely, the will to have a share in the realization of a social project; and this will is all too frequently coerced into the dogmatism of some organization felt and believed to be the only right one, the only just and true organization, the binding claims of which sometimes stand in opposition to the free play of relationships between members. (Community of sentiment is hardly ever sufficient to establish community of life; for this a deeper and more vital bond is required.) The Settlement that remains faithful to dogma is threatened with paralysis; one that increasingly rebels against it, with fragmentation; and both lack the corrective, modifying power of insight into conditions. Wherever dogma reigns supreme, isolation of the Settlement is the sole result; the exclusiveness of "the only right form" precludes union even with like-minded establishments, for in every single one of them the "faithful" are completely obsessed with the absolute character of their unique achievement. But equally, wherever dogma retreats, the economic and spiritual seclusion of the Settlement, especially in a strange country, succumbs to the same fate—isolation, lack of connective power, ineffectuality. None of these things would be so important if some great educative force, sustained by a vigorous upsurge of life and fate, could assure to the communal will a lasting victory over the residue of egoism that inevitably goes with it, or rather raise this egoism to a higher form. But usually it is only the case that collective egoism, i.e. egoism with a clear conscience, emerges in place of individual egoism; and if the latter always threatens to disintegrate the inner cohesion of the community, the former, which is often tainted with dogmatism, prevents the growth of any real communal education as between one community and another, between the community and the world.

Most of the known experimental Settlements came to grief or petered out—and not, as some think, the communist ones alone. Here we must exempt the individual efforts of various religious sects, efforts whose vitality can only be understood in terms of a particular group's faith and as the partial manifestation of this faith; it is characteristic that the federative form makes its appearance here and here alone, as, for instance, with the Russian sect of the Dukhobors in Canada or the "Hutterite Brothers". It is, therefore, unjust of Kropotkin to trace the collapse of the experimental communist Settlements to the fact that they were "founded on an uprush of religiosity, instead of seeing in the commune simply a mode of consumption and production economically ordered". For it is precisely where a Settlement comes into being as the expression of real religious exaltation, and not merely as a precarious substitute for religion, and where it views its existence as the beginning of God's kingdom—that it usually proves its powers of endurance.

Among the causes which Kropotkin adduces for the collapse of most of the Settlements two are worthy of particular note, though at bottom they are one and the same: isolation from society and isolation from each other. He is in error when he imputes the cause to the smallness of the Commune, thinking, as he says, that in such a Commune its members would acquire a distaste for one another after a few years of living together so closely: for, among the Settlements that have lasted at all, we find small ones as well as large ones. But he is right to demand federation to make up for the smallness of the groups. The fact that federation enables members to pass from one settlement to another (which is of crucial importance for Kropotkin), is in reality only one among its many favourable results; the vital thing is federation itself, the complementing and helping of each group by the others, the stream of communal life flowing between them and gathering strength from each. No less important, however, is the fact that the Settlements stand in some relation, if a varying one, to society at large—not merely because they need a market for their surplus production, not merely because youth, as Kropotkin points out, does not tolerate being cut off, but because the Settlements must, in so far as they do not possess that specifically Messianic faith, influence the surrounding world in order to live at all. Whoever bears a message must be able to express it, not necessarily in words, but necessarily in his being.

To a query coming from Settlement circles Kropotkin once answered with an open letter to all Settlement-minded groups stressing the fact that any commonwealth worthy the name must be founded on the principle of association between independent families that join forces. What he meant was that even the individual group must spring from a union of the smallest communal units, federatively. If the federative movement is to extend beyond the group, space is needed: "The experiment," he says in his book *Modern Science and Anarchy*, "must be made on a definite *territory*." He adds that this territory must comprise both town and country. Once more economic motifs have to be geared to the great social motif; genuine community-life means the full play of all the functions and interaction between them, not restriction and seclusion. But it is not enough, as Kropotkin seems to assume that it is, for a town "to make itself into a commune"; if it confronts the finely articulated federation of villages as an unco-ordinated and socially amorphous entity, it is bound to exert rather a negative influence in the long run. It has to co-ordinate itself, convert itself *as a federation* into societies in order to engage in really fruitful intercourse with the villages. Already we can see significant moves in this direction in the "planned economy" theories of our time, the result, mostly, of technical and managerial considerations.

From their long and instructive history we can only give here one characteristic example of the problematical career of the many experimental Settlements to date—Owen's first establishment in this kind, the only one that was his own work: New Harmony in Indiana. He bought the property from the sect of "Separatists" that had immigrated from Germany; after twenty years of work they had managed to make it produce a few blossoms. Members were accepted unselectively; the important German political economist Friedrich List noted at the time in his American Diary: "The elements don't seem to be of the best." In the beginning the Constitution of the new community was based on complete equality between members, for which reason it was also called "The Community of Equality". Two years later, after a number of separate groups had branched off, an attempt had to be made to transform the community into an association of little societies. But this and similar plans for conversion failed. When Owen, returning from a journey to England, saw the Settlement again after it had lasted three years, he had to confess that "the attempt to unite a number of strangers not previously educated for the purpose, who should live together as a common family, was premature", and that "the habits of the individual system" die hard. By selling one part of the land in lots and leasing another in the same way—the experiment cost him a fifth of his fortune —he replaced the Society by a complex of Settlements run on private capitalist lines, only giving them this piece of advice by the way: "To unite their general labour, or to exchange labour for labour on the terms most beneficial for all, or to do both or neither, as their feelings and apparent interests may influence them."

Here we have an example of a Settlement that came to grief not on dogma—despite his definite plans Owen did not commit himself on this point—but rather on the lack of any deep, organic bond between its members.

As an example of the opposite we may cite the development

of Cabet's "Icaria". Undertaken as an attempt to realize a dilettante but successful Utopian novel, born after terrific disappointments and privations and, like Owen's Settlement, the former property of a sect—this time that of the Mormons— the Settlement, during the half-century from its beginnings right up to its final ramifications, underwent schism after schism. First of all there was a schism because Cabet (a temperamental and honestly enthusiastic man, but mediocre) made a bid for dictatorship in the form of dogmatic planning, a bid which kindled a civil war of vituperation and fisticuffs. Of the two groups to which the schism gave rise, the first crumbled into nothing after Cabet's death; in the second a new schism sprang up between the "Young" and the "Old", the "young" championing the dogmatic plan to abolish, for instance, the little gardens that surrounded the houses where the members could pluck not only flowers but fruit as well. Here indeed was a deplorable "remnant of individualism". The affair—after being judicially decided—resulted in the division of the Settlement, the part that contained buildings put up by the "Old" with their own hands being allotted to the "Young". The part remaining to the "Old" lasted another twenty years and then died of "senile decay". The economic forces were strong enough to survive, but the power of belief was extinguished. "We were so few and so like the people outside," writes a female member, "that it was not worth the effort to live in the community." The "Young" Settlement was even shorter-lived. After all kinds of difficulties they moved to California, but under the new organization the principle of private ownership took a significant place, so that the Settlement has not unjustly been compared with a joint-stock company; it soon disbanded itself, the appreciation of land-values being a determining factor, perhaps. So the career of Icaria runs in a strange sequence of dogmatism and opportunism. "We had a furious will to succeed," wrote one of the members several years later, "but the garment we wore was too heavy for us and too long, it trailed at times in the mud; by which I mean to say that the Old Adam in us, or the beast, inadequately repressed, made a violent appearance." But it was not the beast at all, it was only the specifically human species of egoism.

Let us look, finally, at the three chief kinds of "Society" from the point of view of social restructure.

By far the most powerful of them historically, the Consumer Co-operative Society, is least suited in itself to act as a cell of social reconstruction. It brings people together with only a minimal and highly impersonal part of their total being. This part is not, as might be supposed at first glance, consumption. Common consumption as such has a great power to unite people; and, as we know from ancient times, there is no better symbol of communal life than the banquet. But the Consumer Co-operative is concerned not with consumption proper but with purchases for consumption. Common purchasing as such lays no very significant demands on the individuals participating in it, unless it be in exceptional times when it is a question of common care and responsibility for a common task, as in the "heroic" age of the Co-operative Movement or in the crises since then, when private persons came forward in a spirit of sacrifice to alleviate the distress of the many. Similarly, as soon as common purchasing becomes a business, responsibility for which passes to the employees, it ceases to unite people in any significant sense. The bond becomes so loose and impersonal that there can be no question of communal cells and their association in a complex organic structure, even if the co-operative organization of this or that branch of production is linked up with the Co-operative's warehouses. I find this view expressed with great clarity in a book by the Irish poet George William Russell ("A. E."), *The National Being;* a book written with true patriotism and dealing with the social reconstruction of Ireland. He says: "It is not enough to organize farmers in a district for one purpose only—in a credit society, a dairy society, a fruit society, a bacon factory, or in a co-operative store. All these may be and must be beginnings; but if they do not develop and absorb all rural business into their organization they will have little effect on character. No true social organism will have been created. If people unite as consumers to buy together they only come into contact on this one point; there is no general identity of interest. If co-operative societies are specialized for this purpose or that—as in Great Britain or on the Continent—to a large extent the limitation of objects prevents a true social organism from being formed. The latter has a tremendous effect on human character. The specialized Society only develops economic efficiency. The evolution of humanity beyond its present level depends absolutely on its power to unite and create true social

organisms." That precisely is what I understand by an organic
re-structuring of society.

The Producer Co-operative is better suited in itself than the
Consumer Co-operative to take part in a restructuring of this
sort, i.e. to function as the cell of a new structure. Common
production of goods implicates people more profoundly than
a common acquisition of goods for individual consumption; it
embraces much more of their powers and their lifetime. Man
as producer is by nature more prepared to get together with his
kind in an eminently active way than man as consumer; and is
more capable of forming living social units. This is true of the
employer, if and in so far as he draws more strength from the
association for the discharge of his productive activity than he
did and ever could as an individual. But it is particularly true
of the employed, because only in and through the association
does he draw any strength at all—the question is whether he
will become vitally conscious of this opportunity and believe in
its practical prospects. But as we have seen, he succumbs very
easily, indeed almost with a kind of fatality, to the desire to get
others to work for him. If the Consumer Co-operative adapts
itself outwardly, in a technical and managerial sense, to the
capitalistic pattern, the Producer Co-operative does so inwardly
in a structural and psychological sense. At the same time the
latter is itself more amenable to a genuine, not merely technical,
federation; but just how little the paramount importance—
from the point of view of re-structure—of small organic units
and their organic-federative growth was recognized (even in
those circles most enthusiastic for the regeneration of society by
means of Producer Co-operatives), we actually saw two decades
ago in the English Guild Socialist Movement. On the one hand
the bold step was conceived of converting the State into a dual
system: multiform, co-ordinated representation of producers,
and uniform, mass-representation of consumers. But on the
other hand, there soon manifested itself a Saint-Simonistic
tendency aiming at "national" (i.e. embracing a whole branch
of industry) guilds for "the regimentation into a single fellowship of all those employed in any given industry", which proved
much stronger than the tendency to form "local" guilds,
i.e. small organic units and their federation. If the principle of
organic re-structuring is to become a determining factor the
influence of the Full Co-operative will be needed, since in it
production and consumption are united and industry is com-

plemented by agriculture. However long it may take the Full Co-operative to become the cell of the new society, it is vitally important for it to start building itself up now as a far-reaching complex of interlocking, magnetic foci. A genuine and lasting reorganization of society from within can only prosper in the union of producers and consumers, each of the two partners being composed of independent and homogeneous co-operative units; a union whose power and vitality for socialism can only be guaranteed by a wealth of Full Co-operatives all working together and, in their functional synthesis, exercising a mediatory and unifying influence.

For this it is necessary, however, that in place of all the isolated experiments (condemned in the nature of things to isolation) that have made their appearance in the course of more than a hundred years of struggle, there should emerge a network of Settlements, territorially based and federatively constructed, without dogmatic rigidity, allowing the most diverse social forms to exist side by side, but always aiming at the new organic whole.

VIII

MARX AND THE RENEWAL
OF SOCIETY

WE have seen that it is the goal of Utopian socialism so-called to substitute society for State to the greatest degree possible, moreover a society that is "genuine" and not a State in disguise. The prime conditions for a genuine society can be summed up as follows: it is not an aggregate of essentially unrelated individuals, for such an aggregate could only be held together by a "political", i.e. a coercive principle of government; it must be built up of little societies on the basis of communal life and of the associations of these societies; and the mutual relations of the societies and their associations must be determined to the greatest possible extent by the social principle—the principle of inner cohesion, collaboration and mutual stimulation. In other words: only a structurally rich society can claim the inheritance of the State. This goal can be attained neither by a change in the order of government, i.e. those who dispose of the means of power, alone; nor by a change in the order of ownership, i.e. those who dispose of the means of production, alone; nor yet by any laws and institutions governing the forms of social life from outside, alone—nor by a combination of all these. All these things are necessary at certain stages of the transformation, with the restriction, of course, that no coercive order shall result which would standardize the whole and not tolerate the emergence of those elements of spontaneity, internal dynamism and diversity so indispensable to the evolution of a genuine society. What, however, is essential, so essential that all these phases should only subserve its full implementation, is the growth of the genuine society itself, partly from already existing societies to be renewed in form and meaning, partly from societies to be built anew. The more such a society is actually or potentially in being at the time of the changes, the more it will be possible to realize socialism as an actuality in the changed order, that is, to obviate the danger of the power-principle—be it in political or economic form or both—finding entry again, and of the human relations—the real life of society—remaining, underneath the changed surface of laws and institutions, as hopelessly out of joint and askew as ever they were under the capitalist régime. Those changes in the economic and political order inevitably imply, as regards the realization of socialism, the necessary removal of obstacles, but no more and no less. Without such a change the realization of socialism remains nothing but an idea, an impulse and an isolated experiment; but without the actual re-structuring of society the change of order is only a façade. It is not to be supposed that the change comes first and the re-structuring afterwards; a society in transformation may well create for itself the instruments it needs for its maintenance, for its defence, for the removal of obstacles, but changed power-relations do not of themselves create a new society capable of overcoming the power-principle. "Utopian" socialism regards the various forms of Co-operative Society as being the most important cells for social re-structure; and the more "Utopianism" clarifies its ideas the more patently does the leading rôle seem to fall to the Producer-cum-Consumer Co-operative. The Co-operative is not an end in itself for the "Utopian", not even when a large measure of socialism has been successfully realized within it; the point is rather to produce the substance which will then be released by the new order, established in its own right so as to unify the multifarious cells. Genuine "utopian" socialism can be termed "topical" socialism in a specific sense: it is not without *topographical* character, it seeks to realize itself in a given place and under given conditions, that is, "here and now", and to the greatest degree possible here and now. But it regards the local realization (and this has become increasingly clear as the idea has developed) as nothing but a point of departure, a beginning, something that must be there for the big realization to join itself on to; that must be there if this realization is to fight for its freedom and win universal validity; that must be there if the new society is to arise out of it, out of all its cells and those they make in their likeness.

Let us, at this juncture, put the decisive questions of means and ends to Marx and Marxism.

Right from his earliest socialistic formulations up to the full maturity of his thought Marx conceived the end in a way that comes very close to "utopian" Socialism. As early as in August, 1844, he was writing (in his essay *Critical Glosses*): "Revolution as such—the overthrow of existing power and the dissolution of the old conditions—is a political act. But without Revolution socialism cannot carry on. Socialism needs this political act in so far as it needs destruction and dissolution. But when its organizing activity begins, when its ultimate purpose, its soul emerges, socialism will throw the political husk away." We must read this in conjunction with the following passage written earlier on in the same year (*On the Jewish Question*): "Only when man has recognized and organized his 'forces propres' as *social* forces [it is therefore not necessary, as Rousseau thinks, to change man's nature, to deprive him of his 'forces propres' and give him new ones of a social character] and, consequently, no longer cuts off his social power from himself in the form of political power [i.e. no longer establishes the State as the sphere of organized rule] only then will the emancipation of mankind be achieved." Since Marx is known even in his early days to have regarded politics as obviously nothing but the expression and elaboration of class-rule, politics must accordingly be abolished with the abolition of the latter: the man who is no longer "sundered from his fellow-man and from the community" is no longer a political being. This, however, is not regarded as the first consequence of some post-revolutionary development. Rather, as is clearly stated in both the above passages, Revolution as such, i.e. Revolution in its purely negative, "dissolvent" capacity, is the last political act. As soon as the organizing activity begins on the terrain prepared by the overthrow, as soon as the positive function of socialism starts, the political principle will be superseded by the social. The sphere in which this function is exercised is no longer the sphere of the political rulership of man by man. Marx's dialectical formulation leaves no doubt as to what the sequence of events actually is in his opinion: first the political act of *social* revolution will annihilate not merely the Class State, but the State as a power-formation altogether, whereas the *political* revolution was the very thing that "constituted the state as a public concern, that is, as the real State". On the other hand, "the organizing activity" will begin, i.e. the reconstruction of society, only after the complete overthrow of existing power—whatever organizing activity preceded the Revolution was only organization for the struggle. From this we can see with the greatest clarity what it is that connects Marx with "utopian" socialism: the will to supersede the political principle by the social principle, and what divides him from it: his opinion that this supersession can be effected by exclusively political means—hence by way of sheer suicide, so to speak, on the part of the political principle.

This opinion is rooted deep in Marx's dialectical view of history, which found classical formulation fifteen years later in the preface to his book *A Critique of Political Economy*.

Yet, in the concluding section of his polemic against Proudhon, we encounter what appears to be a not inconsiderable limitation. "The working-class," he says, "will, in the course of its development (dans le cours de son développement), replace the old bourgeois society by an association which will exclude classes and their antagonisms, and there will no longer be any political power in its proper sense (il n'y aura plus de pouvoir politique, proprement dit), since political power is nothing but the official sum (le résumé officiel) of the antagonisms obtaining in bourgeois society." "No political power in its proper sense"—that means: no political power in the sense of an expression and elaboration of class-rule, which is quite self-evident if class-rule really has been abolished. Let us leave aside for the moment the question which obviously never entered into Marx's field of vision, namely, whether in those circumstances the proletariat would really be the "last" class, with whose accession to power class-rule would collapse altogether, that is, whether a new social differentiation would not arise within the victorious proletariat itself, one which, even though the class-designation might not apply, might very well lead to a new system of domination. There still remains, however, the no less momentous question as to the nature and extent of political power in the "improper" sense, that is to say, the political power that no longer rests on class-rule but persists after the classes have been abolished. Might it not be possible for such power to make itself no less felt, indeed more felt, than that based on class-rule, especially so long as it was a matter of "defending the Revolution"—so long, in fact, as humanity as a whole had not abolished class-rule, or even, perhaps, so long as humanity had not adopted the view or the realization of socialism prevailing in that particular State in

which the victory of the proletariat had been won? But the
thing that concerns us most of all is this: so long, in such a
State or States, as this fixed point of view prevails, and prevails
with all the technique and instruments of power at the disposal
of our age, how can that spontaneity, that free social form-
seeking and form-giving, that unfettered power of social
experimentation and decision so indispensable to the realization of socialism and the emergence of a socialist form of
society—how can they possibly get to work? By omitting to
draw a clear line of demarcation between power in its proper
and improper senses Marx opens the door to a type of political
principle which, in his opinion, does not and cannot exist:
a type which is not the expression and elaboration of class-rule,
but is rather the expression and elaboration of power-tenden-
cies and power-struggles not characterized by class, on the
part of groups and individuals. Political power in the improper sense would accordingly be "the official sum of
antagonisms" either within the proletarian class itself or, more
precisely, within the nation in which "class-rule has been
abolished".

His impressions of the problematical revolution of 1848
served to sharpen Marx's critical attitude to experiments in
social re-structure. If the "little experiments, inevitably
abortive" had already been censured in the Manifesto, now
(in the report *The Class War in France* of 1850) "doctrinaire
socialism" was accused of "wishing away the revolutionary
conflict of the classes and the need for it by means of petty
artifices and gross sentimentalities", and (in the *Eighteenth
Brumaire* of 1852) the French proletariat was reprobated for
having partly committed itself to "doctrinaire experiments,
exchange-banks and workers' associations", and thus to a
"movement which, having given up the struggle to overthrow
the old world despite all the means at its disposal, prefers to seek
its own salvation behind society's back, privately, inside the
narrow framework of its existence, and which will thus
necessarily come to grief".

Marx's faith in the impending revolution was still unshaken
at that time, but his confidence in an impending World
Revolution in the full sense of the word began to waver. In
1858 he wrote to Engels: "The difficult question for us is this.
On the continent the Revolution is imminent and will immediately assume a socialist form. But will it not necessarily

be crushed in this small corner of the earth [meaning the continent of Europe!], seeing that over a far greater area the movement of bourgeois society is still in the ascendant?" His doubts
seem to have deepened still more in the following years. On the
other hand he became more and more impressed with the
significance of the extra-revolutionary political struggle. After
another six years this was worked out *inter alia* in the "Inaugural
Address to the International Workers' Association". Having
praised the Ten-Hour-Law as the "triumph of a principle", he
went on to call the rise of the Co-operative Movement "a still
greater triumph for the political economy of labour over the
political economy of capital". The value of these great social
experiments, he said, could not be over-estimated; for the
workers, who had set up co-operative factories without any help
at all, had thereby proved that wage-labour "is destined to give
way to associated labour". The co-operative system, however,
if it was to free the masses, needed "developing on a national
scale and consequently promoting by national means", hence
precisely what Louis Blanc and Lassalle had hoped and striven
for. But such a thing would not be conceded by the big landed
proprietors and the capitalists of their own free will. "Therefore," he ends, it is "the great duty of the working class" to
seize political power. We must give this word "therefore" our
full attention. Labour is to win political power in the parlia-
ments in order to sweep the obstacles out of the way of the
Co-operative Movement. Marx is here ascribing a central
significance to co-operation, and in particular to the Producer
Co-operatives. Although it is stressed, as also in Resolutions
Marx drew up for the Geneva Congress of 1866, that the
Co-operative Movement was not capable of remodelling
capitalist society of itself, it is none the less acknowledged as
the proper way to remodel it, save that for this to succeed the
acquisition of State power by the workers was essential. At this
point Marx comes remarkably close to re-structural thinking in
practice without accepting it in principle. Worthy of mention
in this connection is the fact that he clearly recognizes the
danger of the Co-operatives degenerating into ordinary
bourgeois joint-stock companies, and even recommends the
right remedy: that all the workers employed should receive the
same share.

But less than three months before the opening of the Geneva
Congress for which he drew up this Resolution, Marx wrote to

Engels about the tendencies expressed by the French in a debate of the General Council of the International: "Proudhonized Stirnerism. Splitting everything up into little 'groupes' or 'communes' and then making a 'company' of them, but not a State." It is here that the undercurrent of State Centralism creeps unmistakably into Marx's ideas if only by implication. The federalism of Proudhon he is attacking has not the slightest wish to split everything up into communes, it only wants to confer relatively extensive autonomy on the existing communes and combine them in units, whose own combination would represent a more organic form of community than the existing State. As against this Marx once more holds fast to the State as such.

But now, another five years later, a revolutionary event exerted a new influence on Marx's views, an event stronger than any preceding it and tending in another direction: the Paris Commune. In one of his most significant writings, the address to the General Council of the International on the civil war in France, he sketched a picture of the growth, activities and aims of the Commune. The historical reliability of this picture has been disputed, but that does not concern us here: the picture is a confession and one that is of great importance for our theme, which is the variations in Marx's views concerning the evolution of a new society.

What distinguished the Commune in Marx's eyes *toto genere* from all earlier endeavours, "its true secret", is that it was "essentially a working-class government". That is to be understood literally: Marx means a government not merely appointed by the working-class but also actually and factually exercised by it. The Commune is "the self-government of the producers". Born of universal suffrage and elected by the Parisians themselves, representation of this kind, consisting as it does of members who can be replaced at any time and who are bound by the definite instructions of their electors—such representation "should not be a parliamentary but a working body, executive and legislative at the same time". The same form of organization was to be provided for every commune in France right down to the smallest village. The provincial communes were to administer their common affairs in the district parliament and the district assemblies in their turn were to send deputies to the national delegation. In place of centralized State-power originating from the era of absolute monarchy, "with its omnipresent organs", there would consequently emerge a largely decentralized community. "The few, but important, functions, still left over for a Central Government were to be transferred to communal, i.e. strictly answerable officials." The decentralization, however, would not be a fragmentation but a reconstitution of national unity on an organic basis, and would mean a reactivating of the nation's forces and therefore of the national organism as a whole. "The communal constitution would have rendered up to the body social all the powers which have hitherto been devoured by the parasitic excrescence of the 'State', which battens on society and inhibits its free movement. By this deed alone it would have brought about the regeneration of France." It is obvious that Marx is speaking here not of certain historical State-forms but of the State in general. By becoming something "self-evident" local self-government renders State-power "superfluous". Never did any "utopian" Socialist express himself more radically on this point.

But the political structure of the Commune is, for Marx, only a prelude to the real and decisive thing—the great social transformation to which, with its plans and its dispositions, it would inevitably have led had it not been destroyed. He sees in the Commune "the finally discovered political form, in whose sign the economic liberation of labour can march forward". The Commune wanted "to make individual property a truth, by converting the means of production, land and capital into the mere tools of free and associated labour", and labour amalgamated in Producer Co-operatives at that. "If Co-operative production," Marx cries, "is not to remain a snare and a delusion, if it is to oust the capitalist system, if the Co-operatives as a whole are to regulate national production according to a common plan and thereby take it under their own control— what else would that be, gentlemen, but Communism, and a Communism that is *possible*?" That is, a communism that proves its possibility in the teeth of the widespread notion of its "impossibility". A federalism of communes and Co-operatives —for that is precisely what this picture sketches—is thus acknowledged by Marx as genuine communism. To be sure, he still sets his face against all "Utopianism". The working-class "has no cut-and-dried Utopias to introduce by a plebiscite". The communal and co-operative system which it wants to build up into a new community and a new society, is not a contrivance of the mind: only out of the reality of the association of old and new generations, the reality that is gradually emerging from the nation itself, out of these things alone can the working-class build its work and its house. "It has no ideals to realize, it has only to set free those elements of the new society which have already developed in the womb of the collapsing bourgeois society." Here we have that notion of "development" again, dating from 1847; but this time it is completely unequivocal and indubitably meant in the sense of a pre-revolutionary process, one, moreover, whose nature consists in the formation of small, federable units of men's work and life together, of communes and Co-operatives, in respect to which it is the sole task of the Revolution to set them free, to unite them and endow them with authority. This certainly accords at all points with the famous formula given in the *Critique of Political Economy* twelve years previously, as regards the new and higher conditions of production which, however, will never supplant the old "until the material conditions for their existence have been gestated in the womb of the old society itself". But it is nowhere hinted in the report of the General Council that the Paris Commune miscarried because the gestation had not been completed. And the "elements of the new society" that had developed in the womb of the old, collapsing one—they were for the most part those very Co-operatives which had been formed in France under the influence of "utopian" socialism, just as the political federalism of the communes Marx described had been formed under the influence of Proudhon. These Co-operatives it was that were characterized as "little experiments, inevitably abortive" in the Communist Manifesto; but had the Commune triumphed—and everything in the Report indicates that it could have triumphed but for this or that particular circumstance—then they would have become the cell-substance of the new society.

From this standpoint—i.e. of Marxist *politics of revolution*—statements like the following one by Engels in 1873 can therefore be understood: "Had the autonomists been content to say that the social organization of the future would admit authority only within the bounds unavoidably set by the conditions of production themselves, then we could have agreed with them." As if Proudhon had not time and again emphasized the necessity of constantly setting boundaries between possible decentralization and necessary centralization! Another time

(1874) Engels says—adhering strictly to the formulation Marx gave in the Report of the Commission set up by the Hague Congress in 1872 to examine the activities of the Bakuninists— that all socialists were agreed that the State would wither away as a result of the social Revolution-to-be, and political authority with it; but that the "anti-authoritarians" were wrong to demand "that the political State should be abolished at a blow *before* the social conditions producing it were abolished". "They demand," Engels continues, "that the first act of the social revolution should be the abolition of authority." In actual fact no prudent anti-authoritarian socialist had ever demanded anything but that the revolution should begin by curing the *hypertrophy* of authority, its proliferation, and from then on concentrate on reducing it to proportions that would correspond to the circumstances given at any time. Engels answers the alleged demand as follows: "Have you ever seen a revolution, gentlemen? A revolution is certainly the most authoritarian thing there is." If that means that the revolutionary struggle as such must proceed under far-sighted leadership and strict discipline, so much cannot be doubted; but if it means that in the revolutionary epoch (of which nobody can say when it will end), the whole population is to be limitlessly determined in all branches of its life and thought by one central authoritarian will, then it is inconceivable how such a stage can ever evolve into socialism.

Four years after his paper on the Commune Marx, in a letter sharply criticizing the programme sketched for the Unification Congress of Gotha, set out afresh his misgivings about the Co-operatives, with the obvious political intent of bringing one of the chief points in the programme of the Lassallites into question and thus undermining the possibility of any compromise with them. Certainly Marx was only setting his face against the "establishment of Co-operative Societies with State aid", though allowing Co-operative Production to stand as the socialist goal; but expressions like "specific miracle-cure", "sectarian movement" and even "reactionary workers" in connexion with Buchez' programme are clear enough. Despite that, however, the paragraph dealing with Producer Associations financed out of State Credit was accepted by the Congress.

But nothing affords us a deeper insight into Marx's ambivalent attitude to the question of the internal transformation of society

and the conditions for it than his correspondence with Vera
Zasulitch in 1881.

The publication of these documents by Ryazanov is therefore
particularly valuable, because they acquaint us with Marx's
drafts, some of them very detailed, for his answering letter; as
published the drafts run to more than 900 lines, with
innumerable deletions, emendations, amplifications; the letter
itself runs only to about 40.

Vera Zasulitch, "the woman of the moment, the woman with
a mission," as Stepniak calls her, had written to Marx from
Geneva to ask him, as author of *Capital*, the first volume of
which was "enjoying great popularity in Russia" and was also
playing a part particularly in discussions on the agrarian
question and the Russian village community—to ask him what
he thought about the prospects of the village community in
the future. It was, she said, "a question of life and death" for
the Russian Socialist Party, and on it also depended the personal
fate of the revolutionary Socialists. For, either the village
communities, once free of the excessive taxes and tributes as
well as of the Government's arbitrary dealings, were capable in
themselves of developing in a socialist direction, i.e. of gradually
organizing the production and distribution of goods on a
collective basis, in which case the revolutionary Socialist would
have to "devote all his powers to the freeing of the communities
and their development"—or else, as many people who called
themselves Marxists declared, basing themselves on Marx, the
village community was an "archaic form" condemned by
history and scientific socialism alike to perdition. In that case
the Socialists, who would seek in vain to calculate in how
many decades the land would pass out of the hands of the
Russian peasants into those of the bourgeoisie and in how
many centuries capitalism in Russia might conceivably reach
a stage of development similar to that in Western Europe, would
have to restrict themselves to propaganda among the urban
workers, propaganda which "will continue to pour into the
masses of the peasants who, as a result of the dissolution of the
village community, will be thrown on to the streets of the great
cities in their search for wages". One can see that as a matter
of fact it is nothing less than the decision whether or not the
work of the Socialists in Russia could have any assured future
for the next few generations. Must Russia go the way of
Western Europe where, with the rise of Advanced Capitalism,

the "archaic" forms of community necessarily dissolve of themselves, and is there no alternative but to prepare a class-conscious core of urban proletariat for the still distant time of industrialization? On the other hand if there exists, by reason of her special agrarian institutions, a special way for Russia, quite apart, as it were, from the general dialectics of history, a way by which to imbue the traditional pattern of communal ownership and production with Socialist spirit; if one could, by developing this pattern from within and obtaining a better position for it externally, create an organic social reality which would ripen into the Revolution, and, liberated by the latter and established in full freedom and right, which would thereupon constitute itself as the backbone of the new society—if all this, then there is indeed a great and immediate constructive-revolutionary task which may lead quite soon, perhaps, to the realization of socialism. The decision as to which of the two was the historical truth was left in Marx's hands.

His exertions to give the right answer are of a thoroughness and scrupulosity worthy of admiration. Already before this he had occupied himself with the same knotty problem, and now he attacked it afresh with especial intensity. Again and again we see him cancelling one formulation of great delicacy and precision only to seek another still more adequate. Although but a series of fragmentary sketches these notes seem to me the most important attempt that has been made to grasp synthetically the theme of the Russian village community.

Owing to the paucity of historical material the village community is still one of the least understood departments of ethnic sociology, within which the Russian type, whose development is extremely poorly documented, forms a perplexing chapter. In accordance with the prevailing scientific opinion of his time, Marx was inclined to attribute a very early origin to it. To-day we are wont to regard it as rather late in origin and as an outcome of Russia's fiscal policy. But this is surely not the final word. Research will, I think (as important works of our own day indicate) establish that Marx was not so wrong as people assume and that the fiscal system did not create new social forms, but made use of old ones. But here we have to concern ourselves not so much with historical inquiry as with an inquiry into the socialist prospects of the village community, as Marx saw them.

Marx declared in his drafts, in connexion with a remark of the ethnologist Morgan, that the present crisis of capitalism would end by modern society returning to a higher form of the archaic type of communal ownership and production, that is, by its going over to the communist pattern. Hence we were not to let the word "archaic" alarm us—for in this direction lay the golden opportunity for the Russian village community. It had a big advantage over all other archaic communities of the same type: it alone in Europe had maintained itself on a wide national scale. It would not, therefore, as had been the fate of communal ownership in Western Europe, disappear with social progress. Rather, it might "gradually slough off its primitive characteristics and develop as the direct basis of collective production on a national scale". Marx points out that he had, in his "Capital", confined the "historical fatality" of the accumulation of capital which progressively expropriates all property accruing from personal labour, expressly to Western Europe. Since the land in the hands of the Russian peasants had never been their private property, such a line of development was inapplicable to them. Instead, one needed simply to replace the Government institution of the *Volost*, which "links a fair number of villages together", by a "peasant assembly elected by the commune itself and serving as the economic and administrative organ of their interests". The transition from work in allotments to full co-operative work would easily be accomplished then, in which connexion Marx stresses the familiarity of the peasants with the communal work-contracts of the *Artel*[1] as an added inducement to this. The inevitable economic need for such a process would make itself felt as soon as the village community, freed of its burdens and with more land at its disposal, was in normal circumstances; and as for the necessary material conditions, Russian society, having lived so long at the expense of the peasant, surely owed him the requisite wherewithal for such a transition. It is clear that Marx is thinking of a change that can actually be accomplished in the circumstances given. But on the other hand he draws emphatic attention to a peculiarity of the Russian village community which afflicts it with impotence and makes all historical initiative impossible for it. By this he means its isolation; it is a "localized microcosm", and no connexion exists between the life of one commune and that of the others. In other words, what Marx is really missing without consciously making use of

[1] Described in the next chapter.

the idea, is the trend towards *federation*. This peculiarity, he says, is not to be found everywhere as the characteristic of this type of community; but "wherever it is found it has given rise to a more or less centralized despotism over the communes". Only by means of a general revolt can the isolation of the Russian village community be broken. Its present state is (for reasons which Marx does not specify) economically untenable; "for the Russian communes to be saved a Russian revolution is needed". But the revolution must come in time and it must "concentrate all its powers on securing the free rise of the village community". Then the latter will soon develop "comme élément régénérateur de la société russe et comme élément de supériorité sur les pays asservis par le régime capitaliste".

In the short letter that Marx actually sent to Vera Zasulitch, a single sentence follows the reference to the relevant passages in his *Capital*. The sentence runs: "The analysis given in my *Capital* offers, therefore, no reasons either for or against the viability of the village commune; however, the special study I have devoted to it and the material for which I have sought in the original sources convince me that the commune is the mainstay of social regeneration in Russia, but that, if it is to function as such, one must first of all eliminate the injurious influences which work upon it from all sides, and then secure for it the normal conditions of spontaneous development."

The basis of the argument is so enormously compressed that even the message it manages to convey can hardly be grasped in its proper significance. Evidently this process of compression was inevitable, since in the drafts the pros and cons confronted one another in such a manner as to be irreconcilable in fact if not in appearance. In theory Marx affirmed the possibility of a pre-revolutionary development of the commune in the direction desired, but in practice he made its "salvation" dependent on the timely appearance of the revolution. Here as elsewhere the determining factor is clearly the political element: the fear lest constructive work should sap the strength of the revolutionary impetus. Since, however, the political element in Marx was not offset by any insight into the significance of social re-structure, the pros and cons had ultimately to be replaced by a sentence which could hardly appear to Vera Zasulitch as an answer to her fateful question. Even in his own lifetime Marx, as Tönnies says, was something of an oracle who, on

account of the ambiguity of his answers, was often petitioned
in vain. At any rate Vera Zasulitch, in the answer to her
question as to whether the revolutionary socialist should devote
all his strength to the freeing and developing of the communes,
could have heard no "yes" echoing out of Marx's letter, which
for her was of the highest authority.

Not long afterwards she wrote (in the preface to the Russian
translation of Engels' *Evolution of Socialism from Utopia to Science*,
published in 1884) a few passages on the village community
which draw the conclusion from Marx's oracle: that the gradual
liquidation of communal ownership was inevitable; that
Russia's immediate future belonged to capitalism, but that
the socialist revolution in the West would put a term to
capitalism in the East as well, "and then the remnants of
the institution of communal ownership would render a great
service to Russia". In his Foreword to the Russian translation
(also by Vera Zasulitch) of the Communist Manifesto in 1882,
Engels had given a somewhat different answer to the question
he himself formulated obviously under the influence of Marx.
"Can the Russian village community," he asked, "which is
already an extremely corrupt form of the original communal
ownership of land, pass over *direct* to a higher, communist form
of ownership—or must it first of all go through the process of
liquidation familiar to us in the historical development of the
West?" His answer (as usual, less equivocal and more massive
than Marx's, but also less regardful of the profundity of the
problem) is as follows: "Should the Russian Revolution become
the signal for a workers' revolution in the West, so that both
complement one another, then the Russian communal ownership of to-day might serve as the starting-point for communist
development." Later he seems to have grown more sceptical,
but he avoided (so Gustav Mayer reports) "getting involved in
the internal struggles between those Russian Socialists who
trusted more to the peasants and those who trusted more to
the rise of an industrial proletariat".

As against Eduard Bernstein, who rightly pointed out the
similarity between the programme of the Paris Commune as
reported by Marx and Proudhon's federalism, Lenin declared
emphatically that Marx was a centralist and that his statements
in the *Civil War in France* show "no trace of a deviation from
centralism". Stated in such general terms this view is untenable. When Marx says that the few functions "which will then

remain for centralization" should be handed over to communal officials, he means without a doubt: decentralize as many State-functions as possible and change those that must remain centralized into administrative functions, not, however, only *after* some post-revolutionary development lasting an indefinite time, but *inside* the revolutionary action itself—thus realizing what, according to Engels' well-known criticism of the draft to the Erfurt programme, "every French department, every parish possessed: complete self-administration". Nevertheless, Lenin was not wrong; Marx always remained a centralist at heart. For him the communes were essentially political units, battle-organs of the revolution. Lenin asks, "If the proletariat were to organize itself absolutely freely into communes, and were to unite the activities of these communes in a common front against Capital . . . would that not be . . . proletarian centralism?" Of course it would, and to this extent Lenin and not Bernstein is Marx's faithful interpreter. But that is true merely of the revolution as such, which—in the sense of Marx's definition of the commune—is not a "development" spread out over several generations, but a coherent historical *act*, the act of smashing capitalism and placing the means of production in the hands of the proletariat. But in the French programme for the communes each individual commune with its "local self-government" is by no means a mere cog in the great apparatus of revolution, or, to put it less mechanically, not merely an isolated muscle within the revolutionary exertions of the body politic—on the contrary it is destined to outlast the upheaval as an independent unit equipped with the maximum of autonomy. During the act the commune's particular will merges spontaneously in the great impulse of the whole, but afterwards it is to acquire its own sphere of decision and action, so that the really vital functions are discharged "below" and the general administrative functions "at the top". Each commune is already invested in principle with its own proper powers and rights within the revolutionary process, but it is only after the accomplishment of the common act that they can come into actuality. Marx accepted these essential components of the commune-idea but without weighing them up against his own centralism and deciding between them. That he apparently did not see the profound problem that this opens out is due to the hegemony of the political point of view; a hegemony which persisted everywhere for him as far as concerned the revolution, its preparation and its effects. Of the three modes of thinking in public matters—the economic, the social and the political—Marx exercised the first with methodical mastery, devoted himself with passion to the third, but—absurd as it may sound in the ears of the unqualified Marxist—only very seldom did he come into more intimate contact with the second, and it never became a deciding factor for him.

To the question of the elements of social re-structure, a fateful question indeed, Marx and Engels never gave a positive answer, because they had no inner relation to this idea. Marx might occasionally allude to "the elements of the new society which have already developed in the womb of the collapsing bourgeois society", and which the Revolution had only "to set free"; but he could not make up his mind to foster these elements, to promote them and sponsor them. The political act of revolution remained the one thing worth striving for; the political preparation for it—at first the direct preparation, afterwards the parliamentary and trades unionist preparation— the one task worth doing, and thus the political principle became the supreme determinant; every concrete decision about the practical attitude to such re-structural elements as were actually present, in the process of formation or to be constituted anew, was reached only from the standpoint of political expediency. Naturally, therefore, decisions in favour of a positive attitude were tepid, uncoordinated and ineffectual, and finally they were always cancelled out by negative ones.

A characteristic example of the purely political way in which the spiritual leaders of the movement treated the social structures most important for the re-shaping of society, is afforded by Engels' attitude to the Co-operatives. In 1869 (in his preface to the new impression edited by Wilhelm Liebknecht of the paper on the German Peasant War) he had declared: "The agricultural day-labourers can only be redeemed from their misery if the chief object of their work, the land itself, is converted into communal property and cultivated by Co-operatives of Landworkers for the common good." From this fundamental premise he seems to draw a perfectly practical conclusion, when he writes to Liebknecht in 1885 to the effect that the Social-Democratic party of the German Reichstag should say to the Government: "Give us guarantees that the Prussian domains, instead of being leased out to big leaseholders or peasants incapable of living without day-labour, will be leased to Workers' Co-operatives; that public works will be commissioned to Workers' Co-operatives instead of to capitalists—well and good, we will do the rest. If not, not." All these, Engels adds, are things that can be introduced at a day's notice and got going within a year, and are only blocked by the bourgeoisie and the Government. This sounds like genuine demands to be fought for. But in 1886 Engels is demanding of Bebel that the party should propose socialistic measures such as these on the ground that they would conduce to the overthrow of capitalist production; which, therefore, would be a practical impossibility for that Government as for any other bourgeois Government. Here the tactical-propagandist character of the demands is laid bare: the Co-operative principle is merely made use of, not propounded in all seriousness as something simply to be striven and fought for. The tactical application would not be so bad if only the fundamental thing were put boldly and clearly in words: but that is not the case. I cannot help seeing Lassalle's belief—shortsighted as it was—in the practical possibility of Co-operatives with Government aid, as the more socialistic attitude.

As another example of how the leaders' lack of principle on the subject of re-structure led to the sterility of the movement in this respect, I will again give a characteristic sequence of resolutions passed by the Party held to be the most knowledgeable in Marxist matters—the German Social Democrats—anent their relations to the Co-operative. In the Gotha Unification programme of 1875 (concerning the draft of which Marx had voiced his misgivings as mentioned above) it had been demanded that Producer Co-operatives should be set up for industry and agriculture "of such scope that they would result in the socialist organization of all Labour". This was a clear avowal of the re-structural principle, as appeared to be necessary for union with the Lassallites. But in the Erfurt programme of 1891 nothing more was heard of it—which is not to be explained solely by the failures of the Worker and Producer Co-operatives founded in the meantime, but principally by this same lack of fundamental directive, and at the Berlin Party Congress of 1892 it was decided that the Party "could only approve the founding of Co-operatives in so far as they were designed to enable comrades, on whom disciplinary punishment had been inflicted in the political or trades-union struggle, to live a decent social life, or in so far as they served to facilitate agitation"; for the rest, "the Party was opposed to the founding of Co-operatives". This is refreshingly outspoken. But in the resolution of the Hanover Party Congress in 1899 it was stated that the Party was neutral as regards the founding of Industrial Co-operatives, that it saw in the founding of such Co-operatives a suitable means of educating the working-class to the independent control of their affairs, but that it attributed to the Co-operatives "no decisive significance in the matter of freeing the working-class from the chains of wage-slavery". Yet in Magdeburg in 1910 the Consumer.Co-operatives were not merely acknowledged as effectively supporting the class-struggle, it was also declared that Co-operative activity in general was "an effective complement to the political and trades-union struggle to raise the position of the working-class".

This zig-zag line may well serve as a symbol of the tragic mis-development of the Socialist Movement. With all the powerful forces of propaganda and planning it had gathered the proletariat about itself; in the political and economic field it had acted with great aggressive aplomb in attack and defence, but the very thing for which, ultimately, it had made propaganda and planned and fought—the evolution of the new social form —was neither the real object of its thought nor the real goal of its action. What Marx praised the Paris Commune for, the Marxist movement neither wanted nor achieved. It did not look to the lineaments of the new society which were there for all to see; it made no serious effort to promote, influence, direct, co-ordinate and federate the experiments that were in being or about to be; never by consistent work did it of its own accord call any cell-groups and associations of cell-groups of living community into existence. With all its great powers it lent no hand to shaping the new social life for mankind which was to be set free by the Revolution.

IX

LENIN AND THE RENEWAL
OF SOCIETY

JUST as the principle of the renewal of society from within, by a regeneration of its cell-tissue, found no fixed place derivable from the idea itself, in Marx's doctrine, so there was no place for it in the most tremendous attempt of our time to realize this doctrine through the admirable but highly problematical application of conscious human will. In both cases this negative fact can, as we have seen, be justified as regards the pre-revolutionary era by saying that under the reign of capitalism no social regeneration whatsoever, even if only fragmentary, could be accomplished; but as regards the post-revolutionary era it is stated in both cases that it would be "utopian" to outline the appropriate forms of this regeneration. "Utopia," Engels writes in 1872, "arises when, 'from the existing conditions', people undertake to prescribe the form wherein this, that or the other contradiction in existing society will be resolved." "In Marx," says Lenin, "you will find no trace of Utopianism in the sense of inventing the 'new' society and constructing it out of fantasies." But useless as such fantasy-pictures indeed are, it is also of vital importance to let the idea to which one clings dictate the direction towards which one may actively strive. The socialist idea points of necessity, even in Marx and Lenin, to the organic construction of a new society out of little societies inwardly bound together by common life and common work, and their associations. But neither in Marx nor Lenin does the idea give rise to any clear and consistent frame of reference for action. In both cases the decentralist element of re-structure is displaced by the centralist element of revolutionary politics.

In both cases the operative law is that strictly centralist action is necessary to the success of the revolution, and obviously there is no small truth in this; what is wanting is the constant drawing of lines of demarcation between the demands of this action and—without prejudicing it—the possible implementation of a decentralized society; between what the execution of the idea demands and what the idea itself demands; between the claims of revolutionary politics and the rights of an emergent socialist life. The decision always falls—in the theory and directives of the movement with Marx, in the practice of revolution and the reordering of the State and economics with Lenin—essentially in favour of politics, that is, in favour of centralization. A good deal of this can certainly be attributed to the situation itself, to the difficulties which the Socialist movement had to face and the quite special difficulties faced by the Soviet régime; but over and above that a certain conception and a certain tendency subsequently came to the fore which we may find in Marx and Engels and which thereafter devolved upon Lenin and Stalin: the conception of one absolute centre of doctrine and action from which the only valid theses and the only authoritative decrees can issue, this centre being virtually a dictatorship masked by the "dictatorship of the proletariat"— in other words: the tendency to perpetuate centralist revolutionary politics at the cost of the decentralist needs of a nascent socialist community. It was easy for Lenin to give way to this tendency because of the situation itself, which clearly pointed to the fact that the Revolution had not yet reached its end. The contradiction between Marx's demand for the supersession of the political by the social principle on the one hand and the incontestible persistence of it on the other, is disguised and justified by the alleged incompleteness of the revolution; but this does not, of course, take into account the circumstance that for Marx socialism was to slough off its political skin the moment "its organizing activity *begins*". Here there lurks a problem which in its turn is masked by nothing less than the materialistic interpretation of history: according to this view, politics is merely the exemplification and expression of the class-struggle, and with the abolition of the class-state the ground will consequently be cut from under the political principle. The life-and-death struggle of the sole valid doctrine and sole programme of action against all other versions of socialism cannot pass itself off as unpolitical; it must, therefore, brand every other kind of socialism as bogus, as a vestige of bourgeois ideologies; for so long as any other version of socialism exists the Revolution cannot yet be at an end, obviously, and the political principle cannot yet have been superseded by the social, although the organizing activity has already begun. Political power "in the improper sense" can indeed become far more comprehensive, ruthless and "totalitarian" in its centralist pretensions than political power "in its proper sense" ever was. This is not to say that Lenin was a centralist pure and simple: in certain respects he was less so than Marx and in this he was closer to Engels; but in his thought and will the revolutionary-political motif dominated as with Marx and Engels and suppressed the vital social motif which requires decentralized community-living, with the result that this only made itself felt episodically. The upshot of all this was that there was no trace in the new State-order of any agency aiming at the liquidation of State centralism and accumulation of power. How such a liquidation was ever to take place by degrees in the absence of such an agency is inconceivable. Lenin once remarked, in 1918: "What Socialism will be we just don't know. When has any State begun to wither away?" And in history there is indeed no example, however small, to which one could refer. To achieve this for the first time in the world's history one would have needed to set about it with a tremendously vital and idealistic store of decentralizing energy. No such thing happened. That under these circumstances a voluntary renunciation of accumulated power and a voluntary liquidation of centralization would ever take place has not unjustly been characterized (by a Socialist) as a belief in miracles.

The doctrine of the "withering away" of the State after the social revolution was elaborated by Engels from Marx's for the most part very tentative adumbrations. It would not be unprofitable to bring his chief utterances on this subject together in chronological sequence. In 1874 he declared that the State, "as a result of the social revolution of the future, would vanish" because all public functions would simply be changed from political into administrative ones. In 1877 he said more precisely that the proletariat, by converting the means of production into State property, would abolish the State as State and that, moreover, this same seizure of the means of production would "at once be its last independent act as a State", that it would then "fall asleep" or "wither away of itself". In 1882 there follows the eschatological interpretation of this "at once":

there would be the "leap of humanity out of the realm of necessity into the realm of freedom"; nothing could be more outspoken than this. Now, however, a remarkable retreat ensues. After Marx's death we hear no more of this "at once" from Engels' lips. When he announces in 1884 that the whole machinery of State will be relegated to the Museum of Antiquities, the date of this singular proceeding is no longer the moment when the means of production have been nationalized, but evidently a much later moment, and evidently the proceedings will be long-drawn, for the authority which undertakes that relegation to the Museum is now "Society, which will organize production anew on the basis of the free and equal association of the producers"—a task only inaugurated, naturally, by the unique act of nationalization. This accords with the formula in the Communist Manifesto about "the course of development", a formula which Engels recalls here; save that there the formula speaks of the concentration of production "in the hands of associated individuals" as being the result of a development in whose train public power would lose its political character. In 1891 Engels retreats still further, so far indeed that no additional retreat is necessary or even possible. The proletariat, he says, victorious in the struggle for mastery, will not be able to avoid "at once paring down the worst aspects of the State, until a new generation grown up in new, free social conditions is capable of putting aside the whole paraphernalia of State." Engels says this in his Foreword to the new edition of Marx's *Civil War in France*, in which the latter had written twenty years previously that the workingclass "will have to go through long struggles, a whole series of historical processes which will completely transform men and circumstances alike". In his Foreword Engels transposes this conception to the post-revolutionary period. But by so doing the cogency of that "at once" is enormously weakened. Not only is it no longer the case that the proletariat will abolish the State as State with the nationalization of the means of production, but also it will, to begin with and right up to the coming of age of the "new generation", merely "pare down" the worst aspects of the State. And yet in that same book Marx had said of the Constitution of the Paris Commune that, had the Commune triumphed, it would have given back to the social body all the powers which hitherto "the parasitic excrescence of the State" had eaten up; consequently he had laid the main stress on the change brought about by the workings of the Commune—hence on the "at once". But now Engels in his Foreword retreats far beyond this. No doubt certain historical experiences were to blame; but that Engels let himself be influenced by them so profoundly is due to the fact that neither with him nor with Marx was there any uniform and consistent ideal aiming at the re-structuring of society or at preparations for the abolition of the State, or any strong and steadfast will for decentralizating action. It was a divided spiritual inheritance into which Lenin entered: socialist revolutionary politics without socialist vitality.

As is well known, Lenin tried to overcome the problematical nature of Engels' doctrine by pointing out with great emphasis that "the abolition" referred to the bourgeois State but that "the withering away" referred to the "remains of the proletarian State system after the Socialist revolution". Further, that since the State as (in Engels' definition) a "special repressive power" was necessary at first for the suppression of the bourgeoisie, it was also essential as the dictatorship of the proletariat, as the centralized organ of its power. That Lenin hit off Marx's (and Engels') intention is indisputable; he rightly quotes the passage in which Marx, in 1852, had characterized this dictatorship as being the transition to a classless society. But for the Marx of 1871 with his enthusiasm for the Commune it was certain that a decentralization would simultaneously be preparing itself in the midst of the centralism necessary for revolutionary action; and when Engels called the nationalization of the means of production an abolition of the State "as State", he meant the all-important process that would be worked out to the full immediately after the completion of the revolutionary act.

Lenin praises Marx for having "not yet, in 1852, put the concrete question as to what should be set up in place of the State machinery after it had been abolished". Lenin goes on to say that it was only the Paris Commune that taught Marx this. But the Paris Commune was the realization of the thoughts of people who had put this question very concretely indeed. Lenin also praises Marx for having "held strictly to the factual basis of historical experience". But the historical experience of the Commune became possible only because in the hearts of passionate revolutionaries there lived the picture of a decentralized, very much "de-Stated" society, which picture they undertook to translate into reality. The spiritual fathers of the Commune had just that ideal aiming at decentralization which Marx and Engels did not have, and the leaders of the Revolution of 1871 tried, albeit with inadequate powers, to begin the realization of that ideal in the midst of the revolution.

As to the problem of action Lenin starts off with a purely dialectical formula: "So long as there is a State there is no freedom. Once there is freedom there will be no more State." Such dialectics obscures the essential task, which is to test day by day what the maximum of freedom is that can and may be realized to-day; to test how much "State" is still necessary to-day, and always to draw the practical conclusions. In all probability there will never—so long as man is what he is—be "freedom" pure and simple, and there will be "State", i.e. compulsion, for just so long; the important thing, however, is the day to day question: no more State than is indispensable, no less freedom than is allowable. And freedom, socially speaking, means above all freedom for community, a community free and independent of State compulsion.

"It is clear," says Lenin, "that there can be no talk of a definite time when the withering away of the State will begin." But it is not at all clear. When Engels declares that, with the seizure of the means of production, the State will in fact become representative of society as a whole and will thereby make itself superfluous, it follows that this is the time when the withering away must begin. If it does not begin then it proves that the withering tendency is not an integral and determining part of the revolutionary action. But in that case a withering away or even a shrinking of the State cannot be expected of the Revolution and its aftermath. Power abdicates only under the stress of counter-power.

"The most pressing and topical question for politics to-day," states Lenin in September, 1917, "is the transformation of all citizens into workers and employees of one big 'syndicate', namely, the State as a whole." "The whole of society," he continues, "will turn into one office and one factory with equal work and equal pay." But this reminds us, does it not, of what Engels said of the tyrannical character of the automatic mechanism of a big factory, that over its portal should stand written: *Lasciate ogni autonomia, voi ch'entrate.* To be sure, Lenin sees this factory discipline only as "a necessary stage in the radical purging of society"; he thinks that it will pass as soon

as "everybody has learnt to manage society's production by
himself", for from this moment the need for any government
whatever will begin to disappear. The possibility that the
capacity for managing production is unequally distributed and
that equal training may not be able to make up for this natural
deficiency, never seems to have entered Lenin's head. The thing
that would meet the human situation much more would be the
de-politicization of all the functions of management as far as
practicable; that is, to deprive these functions of all possibility
of degenerating into power-accretions. The point is not that
there should be only managers and no managed any more—
that is more utopian than any Utopia—but that management
should remain management and not become rulership, or more
precisely, that it should not appropriate to itself more rulership
than the conditions at any time make absolutely necessary (to
decide which cannot, of course, be left to the rulers themselves).

Lenin wanted, it is true, one far-reaching change to take
place "immediately": immediately after they had wrested
political power the workers were to "smash the old apparatus
of bureaucracy, raze it to its foundations, leave not one stone
upon another", and replace it by a new apparatus composed
of these same workers. Time and again Lenin reiterates the
word "immediately". Just as the Paris Commune had done,
so now such measures shall "immediately" be taken as are
necessary to prevent the new apparatus from degenerating into
a new bureaucracy, chief among them being the ability to
elect and dismiss officials and, in Marx's language, to hold
them "strictly answerable". This fundamental transformation
is not, in contra-distinction to all the others, to be left to the
process of "development", it is supposed to be implicit in the
revolutionary action itself as one of its most momentous and
decisive acts. A "new, immeasurably higher and incomparably
more democratic type of State-apparatus" is to be created
"immediately".

On this point, therefore, Lenin held an immediate change in
the social structure to be necessary. He realized that in its
absence, despite all the formidable interventions, the new
institutions, the new laws and new power-relationships, at the
heart of the body politic everything would remain as of old.
That is why, although he was no adherent of any general
decentralist tendency, he was such an emphatic advocate of
this demand for immediate change which, as far as the Paris

Commune was concerned, had been an organic part of the decentralist order of society and which can only be fulfilled in a society pressing towards the realization of this order. As an isolated demand it has not been fulfilled in Soviet Russia. Lenin himself is reported to have said with bitterness at a later phase: "We have become a bureaucratic Utopia."

And yet a beginning had been made with structural transformation, not indeed on Lenin's initiative, although he recognized its importance if not all its potential structural qualities—a peculiarly Russian beginning akin to the proposals of the Paris Commune and one that had tremendous possibilities —namely the Soviets. The history of the Soviet régime so far, whatever else it is, has been the history of the destruction of these possibilities.

The first Soviets were born of the 1905 Revolution primarily as "a militant organization for the attainment of certain objectives", as Lenin said at the time; first of all as agencies for strikes, then as representative bodies for the general control of the revolutionary action. They arose spontaneously, as the institutions of the Commune did, not as the outcome of any principles but as the unprepared fruit of a given situation. Lenin emphasized to the anarchists that a Workers' Council was not a parliament and not an organ of self-administration. Ten years later he stated that Workers' Councils and similar institutions must be regarded "as organs of revolt" which could only be of lasting value "in connexion with the revolt". Only in March, 1917, after the Sovietic pattern had been, in Trotsky's words, "almost automatically reborn" in Russia and after the first reports of the victory of the revolution had reached Lenin in Switzerland, did he recognize in the St. Petersburg Soviet "the germ-cell of a workers' government" and in the Councils as a whole the fruit of the experiences of the Paris Commune. By this he still meant, of course, first and foremost "the organization of the revolution", that is to say, of the "second real revolution" or "organized striking-force against the counter-revolution", just as Marx saw in the institutions of the Commune above all the organs of revolutionary action; nevertheless Lenin described the Councils, which he held to be of the same nature as the Commune, as already constituting "the State we need", that is, the State "which the proletariat needs" or which is "the foundation we must continue to build on". What he demanded immediately after his arrival in Russia was, in opposition to the opinion prevailing in the Workers' Council itself, "a republic of Workers', Landworkers' and Peasants' Deputy Councils throughout the country, from top to bottom". In this sense the Soviet that then existed was, in his view, "a step towards Socialism", just as the Paris Commune had been for Marx—but of course only a political, a revolutionary-political step as that also had been for Marx; an institution, namely, in which revolutionary thinking could crystallize, the "revolutionary dictatorship, that is, a power supported from below by the direct initiative of the masses and not by the law, which was dispensed by a centralized State-power"; in other words, "direct usurpation". The devolution of power on the Soviets still meant for Lenin not only no real decentralization but not even the incentive to the formation of anything of the kind, since the political function of the Soviets was not an integral part of a plan for a comprehensive, organic order that should include society as well as its economy. Lenin accepted the Councils as a programme for action but not as a structural idea.

The utterance Lenin made the day after his arrival, at a meeting of the Bolshevist members of the All-Russian Con-ference of Councils, is characteristic: "We have all clung to the Councils, but we have not grasped them." The Councils, therefore, already had an objective historical significance for him, quite independent of the significance they had for them-selves and for their own members. For the Mensheviks and the social revolutionaries the Councils were what they had been for the former in 1905 and what they in fact more or less were at the time of Lenin's arrival in Russia: organs for the control of Government, guarantees of democracy. For Lenin and his adherents among the Bolsheviks they were very much more—they were the Government itself, the "only possible form of revolutionary Government"; they were, indeed, the new emergent State—but no more than that. That the decentralist form of this State *in statu nascendi* did not disturb Lenin is due to the fact that the only thing to make active appearance in the Councils Movement at this purely dynamic phase of the Revolution was the undivided will to revolution.

The model of the Paris Commune was vitally important for Lenin both because Marx had exemplified through it—and through it alone—the essential features of a new State-order and because Lenin's mind, like that of all the leading Russian revolutionaries, had been lastingly influenced by the revolutionary tradition of France as being the "classic" of its kind. The influence of the great French revolution, the habitual measuring of their own revolution by it and the constant comparison of equivalent stages, etc., were themselves sufficient to exercise a negative effect, particularly as regards the bias towards centralism. But Lenin did not apply the model afforded by the Commune to any general understanding of history. The fact that (as Arthur Rosenberg rightly stresses in connexion with Kropotkin and Landauer) whenever, in history, the masses endeavoured to overthrow a feudal or a centralist power-apparatus it always ended in these same Commune-like experiments, was either unknown to him or did not interest him; still less did he grapple with the fact (although he once spoke of the Soviets being "in their social and political character" identical with the State of the Commune) that in all those experiments *social* decentralization was linked up with political decentralization, if in differing degrees. For him, the only decisive lesson of history was the conviction that hitherto humanity had not brought forth a higher and better type of government than the Councils. Therefore the Councils had to "take *the whole* of life into their own hands".

Naturally Lenin did not fail to realize that the Councils were in essence a decentralist organization. "All Russia," he says in April, 1917, "is already overspread by a network of local organs of self-administration." The specific revolutionary measures—abolition of the police, abolition of the standing army, the arming of the whole population—could also be put into effect by local self-government; and that is the whole point. But that these organs could and should come together as a lasting organism based on local and functional decentralization after the accomplishment of this task, is not so much as hinted at by a single word, apparently not even by a thought. The setting up and strengthening of self-administration has no ultimate purpose or object other than a revolutionary-political one: to make a self-administration a reality means "to drive the Revolution forwards". Admittedly in this connexion a social note is also struck, if only in passing: the village Commune—which, it is said, means "complete self-administration" and "the absence of all tutelage from above"—would suit the peasantry very well (that "nine-tenths of the peasantry would be agreeable to it" was, be it noted by the way, a fundamental error). But the reason for this follows at once: "We must be centralists; yet there will be moments when the task will shift to the provinces; we must leave the maximum of initiative to individual localities. . . . Only our party can give the watchwords which will really drive the Revolution forwards." At first glance it does not seem clear how this obligatory centralism can be compatible with the complete self-administration mentioned above; on closer inspection, however, we remark that this compatibility rests on the fact that the guiding point of view is, purely and simply, the revolutionary-political one or even the revolutionary-strategic one: in this case, too, self-administration is only a component of the programme of action and not the practical conclusion drawn from a structural idea. This more than anything else enables us to understand why the programmatic demand for "the absence of all tutelage from above" (a demand not envisaged for any post-revolutionary development, but as something to be secured in the midst of the revolution and destined to drive it forwards) turned so rapidly into its exact opposite. Instead of the watchword, "We must be centralists, yet there will be moments . . .", a genuinely socialist attitude would have put it the other way round: "We must be decentralists, federalists, autonomists, yet there will be moments when our main task will shift to a central authority because revolutionary action requires it; only we must take care not to let these requirements swamp its objective and temporal frame of reference."

For a clearer understanding of the antagonism between centralism and the above-mentioned "moments" we must realize that in the provinces, as Lenin himself emphasized, "communes are being formed at a great rate, particularly in the proletarian centres", so that the revolution was progressing "in the form of local communes". The "watchwords" corresponded to these facts. A watchword corresponding to this description of the situation, such as "Local Communes, complete regional autonomy, independence, no police, no officials, sovereignty of the armed masses of workers and peasants"— such a watchword, appeal as it might to the experience of the Paris Commune, was and remained a revolutionary-political one; that is, it could not, of its own nature, point beyond the revolution to a decentralized social structure; centralism continued to be its fixed basis. We cannot help being profoundly impressed when we read, in the same draft (of May, 1917), from

which I have quoted just now, of Lenin's demand that the
provinces should be taken as a model and communes formed
of the suburbs and metropolitan areas; but once again
no other *raison d'être* is granted them except to drive the
Revolution forwards and to lay down a broader basis for
"the passing of the total power of the State to the Councils".
("We are now in the minority, the masses do not believe
us as yet," says Lenin at about the same time.) Lenin is
without a doubt one of the greatest revolutionary strategists
of all time; but the strategy of revolution became for him, as
the politics of revolution became for Marx, the supreme law
not only of action but of thinking as well. We might say that
precisely this was the cause of his success; it is certain at any
rate that this fact—together with a tendency to centralism
rooted very deeply in him as in Marx—was to blame for it if
this success did not ultimately contribute to the success of
Socialism.

Nevertheless these words should not be construed to imply
that I would charge the Lenin of 1917 with not intending to
permit the nascent power of the Soviets to continue beyond
the revolution. That would be nonsensical; for did he not
expressly say at the time, in his significant *Report on the Political
Situation*, of the State that would arise when the Councils took
the power into their own hands (a State that "would no longer
be a State in the accepted sense"), that although such a
Power had never yet maintained itself in the world for any
length of time, "the whole Workers' Movement all over the
world was going in that direction?" What I complain of in
Lenin is rather his failure to understand that a fundamental
centralism is incompatible with the existence of such a Power
beyond the Revolution's immediate sphere of action. It is
noteworthy that Lenin says in the same Report that the latter
was a State-form "which represents the first steps towards
Socialism and is unavoidable in the first phases of socialist
society". These words indicate, I think, that it was conceived
of as being only a stepping-stone to a higher, "socialist"
centralism; and doubtless in the field of economics so
vitally important for any final remodelling of society Lenin
saw strict centralism as the goal. At that very meeting he
emphasized that "the French Revolution passed through a
period of municipal revolution when it settled down to local
self-administration", and that the Russian revolution was going

through a similar phase. It is difficult not to think of the extreme centralism that followed this period of the French Revolution.

Viewed from yet another angle Lenin's doctrine of 1917 leads us to the same result. "Private ownership of ground and of land must be abolished," he says. "That is the task that stands before us, because the majority of the people are for it. That is why we need the Councils. This measure cannot possibly be carried through with the old State officials." Such is the substance of the answer which Lenin gives in his political Report to the question: "Why do we want power to pass into the hands of the Workers' and Soldiers' Deputy Councils?" Here the Marxist respect for "circumstances" is carried to doubtful lengths: private ownership of land is to be abolished not to build up Socialism but simply and solely because the majority of the people want it; and the Councils are necessary not to serve as cells of the new society but to execute the measures demanded by the majority. I would like to assume that we would do well not to take this argument of Lenin's too literally.

But only now does Lenin's theory of the Councils enter the decisive phase. The months in which he was preparing, from Finland, the Bolshevist "special action", "the Second Revolution", were at the same time those in which he based his thought as to the function of the Councils primarily and in principle on Marx's idea of the Commune (in his well-known *State and Revolution*), and then expands it in practice, with reference to the action he had prepared (in his most important political essay *Will the Bolshevists Maintain Power?*). The bulk of the former was written in September at the time of the attempted counter-revolution and its suppression—an attempt whose only effect was to rouse the fighting spirit of the masses and bring them closer to the radical Party; the second in the middle of October, when the majority of the St. Petersburg and Moscow Soviets opted for this party and, as a direct result of this, the call "All Power to the Soviets!", from being a revolutionary-political demand, became the slogan of the impending attack.

Fired by these events, Lenin glorified in his essay the significance of the Councils for the development of the revolution as never before. In connexion with the statement made by the Menshevik leader Martov that the Councils had been "called into being in the first days of the revolution by the mighty outburst of genuine creative folk-power", Lenin says: "Had the creative folk-power of the revolutionary classes [this latter term goes beyond Martov's words and gives them a Bolshevist twist] not produced the Councils, the proletarian revolution in Russia would have been a hopeless affair." Here the conception of the Councils as an instrument for "driving the revolution forwards" struck its most powerful historical note.

In this essay Lenin lists for the first time the various elements which in his view give the Councils their fundamental importance. The sequence in which he cites these elements is characteristic of his outlook.

Firstly, the "new State apparatus", by substituting the Red Guard for the standing Army, invests the people themselves with armed power.

Secondly, it establishes an indissolubly close and "easily controlled" bond between the leaders and the masses.

Thirdly, by means of the principle of eligibility and dismissibility, it puts an end to bureaucracy.

Fourthly, by the very fact that it establishes contact with the various professions [later Lenin puts it more precisely: professions and productive units] it facilitates the weightiest reforms.

Fifthly, it organizes the Avant-garde, which shall raise up and educate the masses.

Sixthly, by means of the tie between the Legislature and the Executive it unites the advantages of Parliamentarianism with those of non-parliamentary Democracy.

The first place is given to revolutionary power-politics; the second to the organization of reforms; the third to the form of the State. The question of the possible importance of the Councils for a reshaping of the social structure is not even asked.

In Lenin's view, however, it only became possible for the Councils to master the tasks set them because the Bolsheviks had seized control in and through the Councils and filled the new form with a concrete content of action, whereas formerly they had been "reduced by the Social Revolutionaries and the Mensheviks to chatter-boxes", more, to "a body rotting on its feet". "The Councils," Lenin continues, "can only really develop, only display their talents and capabilities to the full, after the seizure of supreme power, for otherwise they have nothing to do, otherwise they are either simple germ-cells (and one cannot be a germ-cell for too long) or a plaything." This sentence is remarkable for more than one reason. The simile of the germ-cells necessarily forces the question on us as to whether in Lenin's opinion the Councils might not, by growth and association, ripen sufficiently to become the cells of a renewed social organism; but evidently that is not Lenin's opinion. And then the expression "plaything" turns up again a few days later in a curious connection, in Lenin's theses for a Conference in St. Petersburg, where we read: "The whole experience of the two revolutions of 1905 and 1917 confirms that the Workers' and Soldiers' Deputy Councils are only real as organs of revolt, as organs of revolutionary force. Outside these tasks the Councils are a mere plaything." This makes it unmistakably plain what the important thing really is for Lenin. He had, to be sure, to lay stress on the question of the hour; but the exclusiveness with which he does so, brooking no thought whatever of the Councils eventually becoming independent and permanent entities, speaks a language that cannot be misunderstood. In addition those phrases of 1915 ("organs of revolt" and "only in connexion with the revolt") recur almost word for word; whatever Lenin may have learnt and thought about the Councils during those two years in which he became essentially the historical Lenin, they still remained for him the means to a revolutionary end. That the Councils might not merely exist for the sake of the revolution, but that—and this in a far more profound and primary sense—the revolution might exist for the sake of the Councils, was something that simply never occurred to him. From this point of view—by which I mean not Lenin as a person but the sort of mentality that found an arch-exemplar in him—it is easy to understand why the Councils petered out both as a reality and as an idea.

That Lenin's slogan "All power to the Soviets!" was meant in nothing but a revolutionary-political sense is forced upon us even more strikingly when we come to the following exclamation in that essay: "And yet the 240,000 members of the Bolshevik Party are supposed to be incapable of governing Russia in the interests of the poor and against those of the rich!" So that "All power to the Soviets!" means little more at bottom than "All power to the Party through the Soviets!"—and there is nothing that points beyond this revolutionary-political, indeed party-political aspect to something different, socialistic and structural. Soon afterwards Lenin asserts that the Bolsheviks are "centralists by conviction, by the nature of the programme and the whole tactics of their party"; hence centralism is expressly characterized as being not merely tactical but a matter of principle. The proletarian State, we are told, is to be centralist. The Councils, therefore, have to subordinate themselves to a "strong Government"—what remains then of their autonomous reality? It is true that they, too, are conceded a "special centralism": no Bolshevist has anything to say against their "concentration into branches of production", their centralization. But obviously Lenin had no inkling that such "concentrations" bear a socialist, socially formative character only when they arise spontaneously, from below upwards, when they are not concentrations at all but associations, not a centralist process but a federalist one.

In Lenin's summons "To the People" ten days after the seizure of power we read: "From now on your Councils are organs of State-power, fully authorized to make all decisions." The tasks that were assigned soon afterwards to the Councils referred essentially to control. This was due very largely to the situation itself, but the frame of reference was far too small; the positive counterbalance was missing. Such petty powers were not enough to enable the Councils "to display their talents and capabilities to the full". We hear Lenin repeating in March, 1918, at the Party Congress his ideas about the new type of State "without bureaucracy, without police, without a standing Army", but he adds: "In Russia hardly more than a beginning has been made, and a bad beginning at that." It would be a grave error to think that only the inadequate execution of an adequate design was to blame: the design itself lacked the substance of life. "In our Soviets," he says by way of explanation, "there is still much that is crude, incomplete"; but the really dire and disastrous thing about it was that the leaders, who were not merely political but spiritual leaders as well, never directed the Soviets towards development and completion. "The men who created the Commune," Lenin goes on, "did not understand it." This is reminiscent of his utterance the day after his arrival in Russia: "We have clung to the Councils, but have not grasped them." The truth is that he did not "understand" them even now for what they really were—and did not wish to understand them.

In the same speech Lenin declared in answer to Bukharin, who had demanded that an outline of the socialist order be included in the programme, that "We cannot outline Socialism. What Socialism will look like when it takes on its final forms we do not know and cannot say." No doubt this is the Marxist line of thought, but it shows up in the full light of history the limitations of the Marxist outlook in its relation to an emergent or would-be emergent reality: a failure to recognize potentialities which require, if they are to develop, the stimulus of the idea of social form. We may not "know" what Socialism will look like, but we can know what we want it to look like, and this knowing and willing, this conscious willing itself influences what is to be—and if one is a centralist one's centralism influences what is to be. Always in history there exist, even if in varying degrees of strength, centralist and decentralist trends of development side by side; and it is of vital importance in the long run *for which* of the two the conscious will, together with whatever power it may have acquired at the time, elects. What is more, there is scarcely anything harder, or more rare, than for a will invested with power to free itself from centralism. What more natural or more logical than that a centralist will should fail to recognize the decentralist potentialities in the forms it makes use of? "The bricks are not yet made," says Lenin, "with which Socialism will be built." Because of his centralism he could not know and acknowledge the Councils as such bricks, he could not help them to become so, nor did they become so.

Soon after the Party Congress Lenin stated in the first draft of the *Theses on the Immediate Tasks of Soviet Authority*, in a section not included in the final version: "We are for democratic centralism. . . . The opponents of centralism are always pointing to autonomy and federation as a means of combating the hazards of centralism. In reality democratic centralism in no way precludes autonomy, rather it postulates the need for it. In reality even federation [here Lenin only has political federation in mind] in no way contradicts democratic centralism. In a really democratic order, and all the more in a State built up on the Soviet principle, federation is only a step towards a really democratic centralism." It is clear that Lenin has no thought of limiting the centralist principle by the federalist principle; from his revolutionary-political point of view he only tolerates a federal reality so long as it resolves itself into centralism. The direction, the whole line of thought is thus unequivocally centralistic. Nor is there any essential difference when we come to local autonomy: it is expedient to permit this to a certain degree and to grant it its terms of action; only the line must be drawn at that point where the real decisions and consequently the central instructions begin. All these popular and social formations only have political, strategic, tactical and provisional validity; not one of them is endowed with a genuine *raison d'être*, an independent structural value; not one of them is to be preserved and fostered as a living limb of the community-to-be.

A month after Lenin had dictated his draft the "Left Communists" pointed out how injurious it was for the seeds of Socialism that the form which State administration was taking lay in the direction of bureaucratic centralization, elimination of the independence of the local Soviets and repudiation, in fact, of the type of "Commune-State" governing itself from below—the very type, therefore, of which Lenin said in his speech that the Soviet Authority actually was. There can be no more doubt to-day as to who was right in assessing the situation and the trends to come—Lenin or his critics. But Lenin himself knew it well enough towards the end of his life. References to the Paris Commune become fewer and fewer after that speech, until they cease altogether.

A year after the October Revolution, Lenin had stated that "the apparatus of officialdom in Russia was completely shattered", but at the end of 1920 he characterized the Soviet Republic as "a Work-State with bureaucratic excrescences", and that, he said, "was the truth about the transition". The fact that in the years to come the proportion of excrescences to the trunk from which they sprouted increased alarmingly, and the buddings of the state of affairs to which the transition was supposed to lead grew less and less, could not remain hidden from Lenin. At the end of 1922 in the report *Five years of Russian Revolution and the World Revolution in Perspective* which Lenin made to the Fourth Congress of the Communist International, he says simply: "We have taken over the old State apparatus." He solaces himself with the assurance that in a few years they will succeed in modifying the apparatus from top to bottom. This hope was not fulfilled and could not be fulfilled given Lenin's assumptions: he was thinking in the main of training and attracting new forces, but the problem was one of structure and not of personnel; a bureau-cracy does not change when its names are changed, and even the best-trained graduates of the Soviet schools and Workers' Faculties succumb to its atmosphere.

Lenin's main disappointment was the continued existence of the bureaucracy which, if not in its personnel, certainly in its ruthless efficacy, once more proved stronger than the revolutionary principle. He does not seem to have touched the deeper causes of this phenomenon, and that is understandable enough. The October Revolution was a social revolution only in the sense that it effected certain changes in the social order and its stratification, in the social forms and institutions. But a true social revolution must, over and above that, establish the rights of society *vis-à-vis* the State. Although in respect of this task Lenin pointed out that the withering away of the State would be accomplished by way of a development whose duration could not as yet be measured nor its manner imagined, yet, to the extent that this development could be realized right now, he acknowledged the task as determining the leaders' immediate programme of action and called the new State-form whose realization was to be tackled at once, the "Commune State". But the "Commune State" had been characterized clearly enough by Marx as freeing economic society to the greatest possible extent from the shackles of the political principle. "Once the communal order of things," he wrote, "had been introduced in Paris and in the centres of second rank, the old centralized government would have had to give way in the provinces also to the producers' self-government." This shifting of the power of decision from the political to the social principle—which had been worked out and given its ideal basis in France by the social thinking from Saint-Simon to Proudhon—was proclaimed by Lenin as the base-line for the organizing activity of the leaders, but in point of fact it did not become such a base-line. The political principle established itself anew, in changed guise, all-powerful; and the perils actually threatening the revolution gave him a broad justification. Let it remain undisputed that the situation as it was would not have allowed of a radical reduction of the political principle; what, however, would at any rate have been possible was the laying down of a base-line in accordance with which, as changing circumstances allowed, the power-frontiers of the social principle could have been extended.

Precisely the opposite happened. The representatives of the political principle, that is, mainly the "professional revolutionaries" who got to the top, jealously watched over the unrestrictedness of their sphere of action. It is true that they augmented their ranks with competent persons recruited from the people and that they filled up the gaps as they arose, but those who were admitted to the directorate bore the stamp of the political principle on their very souls; they became elements of the State substance and ceased to be elements of the social substance, and whoever resisted this change could not make himself heard at the top or soon ceased to want to. The power of the social principle could not and dared not grow. The beginnings of a "producers' self-government" to which the revolution spontaneously gave rise, above all the local Soviets, became, despite the apparent freedom of expression and decision, so enfeebled by the all-pervading Party domination with its innumerable ways visible and invisible of compelling people to conform to the doctrine and will of the Central Authority, that little was left of that "outburst of creative folk-power" which had produced them. The "dictatorship of the proletariat" is *de facto* a dictatorship of the State over society, one that is naturally acclaimed or tolerated by the overwhelming mass of people for the sake of the completed social revolution they still hope to see achieved by this means. The bureaucratism from which Lenin suffered, and suffered precisely because it had been his business to abolish it (the "Commune State" being, for him, nothing less than the debureaucratized State), is merely the necessary concomitant to the sovereignty of the political principle.

It is worth noting that within the Party itself attempts were made again and again to break this sovereignty. The most interesting of them, because it sprang from the industrial workers, seems to my mind to be the "Workers' Opposition" of March, 1921, which proposed that the Central Organs for the administration of the whole national economy of the Republic should be elected by the united trades-associations of producers. This was not a Producers' Government by any means but it was an important step towards it, although lacking any real decentralist character. Lenin rejected this "anarcho-syndicalist deviation" on the ground that a union of producers could be considered by a Marxist only in a classless society composed exclusively of workers as producers, but that in Russia at present there were, apart from remnants of the capitalist epoch, still two classes left—peasants and workers. So long, therefore, as Communism was still aiming at perfection and had not turned all peasants into workers a self-governing economy could not, in Lenin's opinion, be considered. In other words (since the completion of Communism coincides with the complete withering away of the State): a fundamental reduction of the State's internal sphere of power cannot be thought of before the State has breathed its last. This paradox has become the operative maxim for the directorate of the Soviet Régime.

Only from this point of view can Lenin's changing attitude to the Co-operative System be grasped as a whole.

There is no point, however, in picking on the contradictions in a critical spirit. Lenin himself emphasized in 1918, not without reason, that always when a new class enters the historical arena as the leader of society there comes unfailingly a period of experiment and vacillation over the choice of new methods to meet the new objective situation; three years later he even asserted that things had only proved, "as always in the history of revolutions, that the movement runs in a zigzag". He failed to notice that though all this may be true of political revolutions, yet when, for the first time in history on so large a scale, the element of social change is added, humanity as a whole (and this means the people to whom events happen as well as the witnesses of them) longs despite all the experiments and vacillations to be made aware of the one clear earnest of the future: the movement towards community in freedom. In the case of the Russian Revolution whatever else may have appeared to them in the way of portents nothing of this kind ever became visible, and Lenin's changing attitude to the Co-operative system is one proof the more that such a movement does not exist.

In the pre-revolutionary period Lenin regarded the Co-operatives existing in bourgeois society as "miserable palliatives" only and bulwarks of the petty bourgeois spirit. A month before the October Revolution, faced with the tremendous economic crisis that was sweeping Russia, he put forward among the "revolutionary-democratic" measures to be taken immediately, the compulsory unification of the whole nation into Consumer Co-operatives. The following January he wrote in the draft of a decree: "All citizens must belong to a local Consumer Co-operative" and "the existing Consumer Co-operatives will be nationalized". In some Party circles this demand was understood and approved as aiming at the elimination of the Co-operatives, for they saw, as a Bolshevist theoretician no doubt rightly expressed it, in the element of *voluntary* membership the essential hallmark of a Co-operative. Lenin did not intend it to be understood that way. True, the Co-operative as a small island in capitalist society was, so he said, only "a shop", but the Co-operative which, after the abolition of private capital, comprises the whole of society "is Socialism", and it is therefore the task of the Soviet authorities to change all citizens without exception into members of a general State Co-operative, "a single gigantic Co-operative". He does not see that the Co-operative principle thereby loses all independent content, indeed its very existence as a principle, and that nothing remains but a necessarily centralist-bureaucratic State-institution under a name that has become meaningless. The realization of this programme was undertaken in the years immediately following: all Co-operatives were merged under the leadership of the Consumer Co-operatives, which were turned into what amounted to State goods-distribution centres. As to immediate nationalization pure and simple, even two years after he had formulated the "Tasks of the Soviet Authority" Lenin was still holding back. He denounced those who were outspoken enough to demand a single nexus of State organizations to replace the Co-operatives. "That would be all right, but it is impossible", he said, meaning "impossible at present". At the same time he held fast in principle to the idea of the Co-operative as such, which, he declared (recalling Marx and his own attitude at the Copenhagen Congress of the International in 1910, where he had stressed the possible socializing influence of the Co-operative after the capitalists had been expropriated), might be a means of building the new economic order. It was therefore a question, he said, of finding new Co-operative forms "which correspond to the economic and political conditions of the proletarian dictatorship" and which "facilitate the transition to real socialist centralism". An institution the very essence of which is the germ and core of social decentralization was in consequence to be made the building element of a new close-meshed State centralism of "socialist" stamp. Obviously Lenin was not proceeding from theoretical assumptions but from the practical requirements of the hour which, as the world knows, were extremely grave and necessitated the most strenuous exertions. When Lenin, in a statement reminiscent of the postulates of the "Utopians" and "Anarchists"—but naturally twisting their meaning into its exact opposite—demanded the union of the Producer and Consumer Co-operatives, he did so because of the need to increase the supply of goods: the fitness of this measure being proved by the experience of the last two years. A year later we hear him polemicizing violently against the Co-operatives, which in their old and still unconquered form were a "bulwark of counter-revolutionary opinion". In his famous treatise on *Taxation in Kind* (spring, 1921) he points emphatically to the danger that lurks in the co-operation of small producers: it inevitably strengthens petty bourgeois capitalism. "The freedom and rights of the Co-operatives," he continues, "mean under present conditions in Russia, freedom and rights for capitalism. It would be a stupidity or a crime to close our eyes to this obvious truth." And further: "Under Soviet power Co-operative capitalism, as distinct from private capitalism, creates a variant of State capitalism and is as such advantageous and useful to us at present. . . . We must endeavour to guide the development of capitalism into the channels of Co-operative capitalism." This instructive warning only expressed what, in those years of falsely so-called "War Communism" (in October, 1921, Lenin himself spoke retrospectively of the mistake that had been made by "our having resolved to take in hand the immediate change-over to communist production and distribution") had been the guiding principle in practice.

But in the wake of the unfavourable outcome of extreme centralization and in connexion with the "New Economic policy" just beginning, a regressive tendency was already making itself felt. Shortly before that warning declaration of Lenin's a decree had been promulgated on the re-establishment of the various kinds of Co-operative—Consumer, Agricultural and Industrial—as an economic organization. Two months later there followed a decree with which a beginning was made for the wholesale cancellation of the previously arranged merging of all Co-operatives in the Association of Consumer Co-operatives, the "Zentrosoyus". Towards the end of the same year the president of this Association declared in a speech on the position and tasks of the Co-operatives that it was only natural that the State Co-operative apparatus, functioning in accordance with a fixed plan, should have become "bureau-cratic, inelastic and immovable", and he made mention of the voices "that spoke of the necessity of freeing the Co-operative from slavery to the State", indeed, he even admitted that there were times "when one had to speak of such a freeing". And true enough the people had often come to compare compulsory organization with bondage. Now the authorities "completely and unreservedly" abjured all official interference in the affairs of the Agricultural Co-operatives and contented themselves with the wide possibilities within the system of State Capital-ism for "influencing and regulating the Co-operatives by eco-nomic pressure", until those that "could not or would not adapt themselves" had been "rubbed out and liquidated". All the same, care was taken that reliable Party members should get into the directorate of the central as well as of the individual Societies and that the necessary "purges" were carried out under the representatives of the Co-operative.

Two years after the appearance of his *Taxation in Kind*, Lenin, in May, 1923, the peak period of the New Economic Development, provided the latter with its theoretical foundation in his great essay on the Co-operative System. "When we went over to the New Economics," he said, "we acted precipitately in one respect, namely, we forgot to think of the Co-operative System." But he no longer contents himself now with approving the Co-operative as a mere element to be built into the State economy of the transition period. All of a sudden the Co-opera-tive is jerked into the very centre of the social new order. Lenin now describes the Co-operative education of the people as "the only task that is left us". The "co-operativization" of Russia has acquired in his eyes a "colossal", a "gigantic", a "limitless" significance. "It is," he says, "not yet the actual building of the socialist society, but it contains everything necessary and sufficient for the building of this society." Yes, he goes even further: the Co-operative has become for him not merely the pre-condition of social building but the very core of it. "A social order of enlightened Co-operatives," he asserts, "with common ownership of the means of production, based on the class-victory of the proletariat over the bourgeoisie—that is a socialist order of society," and he concludes: "The simple growth of the Co-operative is as important for us as the growth of socialism," yes, "conditional to the complete co-operativiza-tion of Russia we would be already standing with both feet on

socialist ground." In the planned, all-embracing State
Co-operative he sees the fulfilment of the "dreams" of the old
Co-operatives "begun with Robert Owen". Here the contradiction between idea and realization reaches its apogee.
What those "Utopians", beginning with Robert Owen, were
concerned about in their thoughts and plans for association
was the voluntary combination of people into small independent units of communal life and work, and the voluntary
combination of those into a community of communities. What
Lenin describes as the fulfilment of these thoughts and plans is
the diametrical opposite of them, is an immense, utterly
centralized complex of State production-centres and State
distribution-centres, a mechanism of bureaucratically run
institutes for production and consumption, each locked into
the other like cog-wheels: as for spontaneity, free association,
there is no longer any room for them whatever, no longer the
possibility of even dreaming of them—with the "fulfilment" of
the dream the dream is gone. Such at any rate had been
Lenin's conception of the dovetailing of the Co-operative
system into the State, and in that otherwise very exhaustive
essay of his written eight months before his death he did not
deny it. He wanted to give the movement which had then
reached its peak and which implied a reduction of centralism
in all fields, a definitive theoretical basis; but he denied it—
necessarily, given his train of thought—the basis of all bases:
the element of freedom.

Some people have thought they could see in this marked
turning of Lenin's towards the Co-operatives an approach to
the theories of the Russian Populists, for whom such forms of
communal association as persisted or renewed themselves
within the body of the people were the core and bud of a future
order of society, and whom Lenin had fought for so long. But
the affinity is only apparent. Even now Lenin was not thinking
for a moment of the Co-operative as a spontaneous, independent formation growing dynamically and a law unto itself.
What he was now dreaming of, after all his grievous efforts to
weld the people into a uniform whole that would follow him
with utter devotion, after all his disappointments over "bureaucratic excrescences", with the mark of illness on him and near
to death—was to unite two things which cannot be united, the
all-overshadowing State and the full-blooded Co-operative, in
other words: compulsion and freedom. At all periods of human

history the Co-operative and its prototypes have been able really to develop only in the gaps left by the effective power of the State and its prototypes. A State with no gaps inevitably precludes the development of the Co-operative. Lenin's final idea was so to extend the Co-operative in scope and so to unify it in structure that it would only differ from the State functionally but coincide with it materially. That is the squaring of the circle.

Stalin has explained the change in Lenin's attitude to the Co-operatives from 1921 to 1923 by saying that State Capitalism had not gained foothold to the degree desired, and that the Co-operatives with their ten million members had begun to ally themselves very closely with the newly developing socialized industries. This certainly draws attention to Lenin's real motives, but it is not sufficient to explain his unexpected enthusiasm for Co-operatives. Rather, it is obvious that Lenin now perceived in the Co-operative principle a counterbalance to the bureaucracy he found so offensive. But the Co-operative could only have become such a counterbalance in its original free form, not in Lenin's compulsory form, which was dependent on a truly "gigantic" bureaucracy.

As we have said, Lenin's idea of compulsion was not carried out to the full. The regressive movement finally led, in May, 1924, to the restoration of voluntary membership, at first only for full citizens, that is, citizens entitled to vote, but later, early in 1928, in the rural Consumer Co-operatives for others as well, although with some limitation as to their rights. Towards the end of 1923 the Board of the Zentrosoyus stated: "We must confess that this change-over to free membership ought to have been made earlier. We could then have met this crisis on a surer foundation." All the same an indirect compulsion was henceforth exercised by means of preferential supplies to the Co-operatives. In 1925 we hear from the mouth of the then president of the Central Council of the Trades Unions that the Government, when issuing subsidies and loans, took account of a person's membership in a manner that came very near to compulsion. And ten years afterwards the urban Co-operatives, which had long suffered gravely under State interference, were abolished at a stroke in 654 cities.

What has been said will suffice to show how the Soviet régime continually oscillated in practice between immediate radical centralization and provisional tolerance of relatively decentralized areas, but never, even to the slightest degree, made the trend towards the goal of Socialism as formulated by Marx, namely, "the sloughing off of the political husk", the maxim of its conduct. One might amplify this by mentioning the changing attitude it adopted during the Five Year Plan of 1926 to 1931 to the collectivization of the peasantry. I shall content myself with listing a few characteristic proclamations and procedures in chronological sequence.

Towards the end of 1927, Molotov drew attention to the backwardness of agriculture and in order to overcome it demanded that the village Collectives—valuable despite their defects—should develop in conjunction with the general plan of industrialization. In June, 1928, Stalin declared it necessary to expand the existing Collectives as intensively as possible and establish new ones. In April, 1929, the slogan was given out at the Party Congress for the creation, still within the framework of the Five Year Plan, of a socialized area of production as a counterbalance to individual economy. The process of collectivization soon took on more or less obvious forms of compulsion and seemed so successful at first that Stalin stated at the end of the same year: "If collectivization goes on at this rate the contrast between town and village will be wiped out in accelerated tempo." At the beginning of 1930 the Central Committee of the Party estimated that the tempo envisaged in the Plan had been outstripped, and emphatically stressed the need for a concerted campaign against all attempts to slow the movement down. In three years' time complete collectivization would have been achieved with the techniques of persuasion, "aided by certain levers". The Executive Committees of the various districts vied with one another in the thoroughness of their administrative measures; a district was not infrequently declared an "area of complete collectivization" and where persuasion did not help threats were used. But it soon proved that the impression of smashing success, an impression fostered by the marked increase in the number of collective farm-economies, was a delusion. The peasants reacted in their own way, by anything from the slaughtering of cattle to actual uprisings, and the measures taken to liquidate the kulaks did little to remedy the evil; the small peasants often joined forces and the Red Army itself with its peasant sons reflected the prevailing dissatisfaction. Then Stalin, in his famous article "Dizzy with Success", performed the volte face that seemed necessary. The policy of collectivization, he declared, rested according to Lenin's doctrine on voluntary action. "You cannot create collective economies by force. That would be stupid and reactionary." Lenin had also taught, he said, that "it would be the greatest folly to try to introduce collective cultivation of the land by decree". The voluntary principle had suffered injury, the tempo of action had not corresponded to that of development, important intermediate stages on the way to the complete Village Commune had been by-passed. The Central Committee was therefore arranging, he said, for an end to be made of compulsory methods. In July the Party Congress proclaimed that collective economies could only be based on the principle of voluntary admission, all attempts to apply force or administrative coercion were "an offence against the Party line and an abuse of power". In the autumn the Commissar for Agriculture once more criticized "the crude and ultra-administrative methods which have been employed in respect of the collective economies and their members". But less than five months later, after a considerable number of peasants, as a result of the greater measure of freedom but in spite of the privileges newly offered, had left the Collectives, the same Commissar said in his Report to the Congress of the Soviets regarding the small and middling peasants who had not joined the Collective Movement: "Who are they for, for the kulaks or for the Collectives? . . . Is it possible to remain neutral to-day?" In other words: he who is not for collectivization is against the Soviet régime. The Congress confirmed this view. During the next few years renewed measures of severity followed the alleviations necessitated by the famine crisis, until in 1936 nearly 90 per cent of the peasants had been collectivized, of which the Full Communes comprised only a diminishing fraction.

The old rustic Russia, as Maynard has rightly said, lasted up to 1929. That it was bundled out of the world with its traditional system of land-cultivation can, from the point of view of economic efficiency, only be approved. But, from the point of view of social structure, the question must be put very differently. From this angle there should be no talk of an Either-Or; the specific task was so to transform the existing structural units that they should be equal to the new conditions and demands, and at the same time retain their structural character and nature as self-activating cells. This task has not been fulfilled. It has been said, rightly enough, that Marxist thinking, geared as it is to the rationalized big-business form of farming, the industrialization and mechanization of agriculture, has been grafted onto the old Russian Village Community which had accustomed the peasants to the communal management of land. But the politically inspired tendency to turn agriculture into a department of industry and the peasants into the hired workers of this industry; the tendency to an all-embracing and all-regulating State economy; a tendency which regards the Agricultural Co-operative only as a stepping-stone to the Full Commune and this in its turn only as a stepping-stone to the local branch of the Agricultural Department of the Universal State Factory—such a tendency destroyed and was bound to destroy the whole structural value of the Village Community. One cannot treat either an individual or a social organism as a means to an end absolutely, without robbing it of its life-substance. "From the standpoint of Leninism," said Stalin in 1933, "the collective economies, and the Soviets as well, are, taken as a form of organization, a weapon and nothing but a weapon." One cannot in the nature of things expect a little tree that has been turned into a club to put forth leaves.

Far longer than with any other people the "medieval" tendency to associate in little bands for the purpose of common work has been preserved among the Russians. Of the most singular social formation to have sprung from this tendency, the *Artel*, Kropotkin could say some forty years ago that it constituted the proper substance of Russian peasant life—a loose, shifting association of fishermen and hunters, manual workers and traders, hauliers and returned Siberian convicts, peasants who travelled to the city to work as weavers or carpenters, and peasants who went in for communal corn-growing or cattle-raising in the village, with, however, divisions as between communal and individual property. Here an incomparable building element lay ready to hand for a great re-structural idea. The Bolshevist Revolution never used it. It had no use for independent small communities. Among the various types of "Kolkhoz" it favoured "for the present", as Stalin said, the agricultural *Artel* for economic reasons, but naturally the revolution saw in it nothing but a stepping-stone. One of Russia's best theoreticians of economics has defined the aim. Land cultivation, he said, would only be regarded as socialized when all the agricultural *Artels* had been replaced by State Collectives, when land, means of production and live-stock belonged to the State. Then the peasants would live in community-houses as hired labourers of the State, in huge agrarian cities, themselves the nodes of areas blessed with more and more electrification. The fantastic picture to which this conception belongs is in very truth the picture of a society finally and utterly de-structured and destroyed. It is more—it is the picture of a State that has devoured society altogether.

The Soviet régime has achieved great things in the technology of economics and still greater things in the technology of war. Its citizens seem in the main to approve of it, for a variety of reasons, negative and positive, fictitious and real. In their attitude vague resignation appears mixed with practical con-fidence. It can be said in general that the individual submits to this régime, which grants him so little freedom of thought and action, perhaps because there is no going back and as regards technical achievements there is at least a going forward. Things look very different, at least to the impartial eye, when it comes to what has actually been achieved in the matter of Socialism: a mass of socialistic expostulations, no Socialist form at all. "What," asked the great sociologist Max Weber in 1918, "will that 'association' look like of which the Communist Manifesto speaks? What germ-cells of that kind of organization has Socialism in particular to offer if ever it gets a real chance to seize power and rule as it wills?" In the country where Socialism did get this chance there still existed such germ-cells, which no other country in our epoch could rival; but they were not brought to fruition. Nevertheless, there is still breathing-space for change and transformation—by which is meant not a change of tactics such as Lenin and his fellow-workers often effected, but a change of fundamentals. The change cannot go backwards, only forwards—but in a new direction. Whether forces as yet unnamed are stirring in the depths and will suddenly burst forth to bring about this change, on this question tremendous things depend.

Pierre Leroux, the man who appears to have used the word "Socialism" for the first time, knew what he was saying when he addressed the National Assembly in 1848 with these words: "If you have no will for human association I tell you that you are exposing civilization to the fate of dying in fearful agony."

X

IN THE MIDST OF CRISIS

FOR the last three decades we have felt that we were living in the initial phases of the greatest crisis humanity has ever known. It grows increasingly clear to us that the tremendous happenings of the past years, too, can be understood only as symptoms of this crisis. It is not merely the crisis of one economic and social system being superseded by another, more or less ready to take its place; rather all systems, old and new, are equally involved in the crisis. What is in question, therefore, is nothing less than man's whole existence in the world.

Ages ago, far beyond our calculation, this creature "Man" set out on his journey; from the point of view of Nature a well-nigh incomprehensible anomaly; from the point of view of the spirit an incarnation hardly less incomprehensible, perhaps unique; from the point of view of both a being whose very essence it was to be threatened with disaster every instant, both from within and without, exposed to deeper and deeper crises. During the ages of his earthly journey man has multiplied what he likes to call his "power over Nature" in increasingly rapid tempo, and he has borne what he likes to call the "creations of his spirit" from triumph to triumph. But at the same time he has felt more and more profoundly, as one crisis succeeded another, how fragile all his glories are; and in moments of clairvoyance he has come to realize that in spite of everything he likes to call "progress" he is not travelling along the high-road at all, but is picking his precarious way along a narrow ledge between two abysses. The graver the crisis becomes the more earnest and consciously responsible is the knowledge demanded of us; for although what is demanded is a deed, only that deed which is born of knowledge will help to overcome the crisis. In a time of great crisis it is not enough to look back to the immediate past in order to bring the enigma of the present nearer to solution: we have to bring the stage of the journey we have now reached face to face with its beginnings, so far as we can picture them.

The essential thing among all those things which once helped man to emerge from Nature and, notwithstanding his feebleness as a natural being, to assert himself—more essential even than the making of a "technical" world out of things expressly formed for the purpose—was this: that he banded together with his own kind for protection and hunting, food gathering and work; and did so in such a way that from the very beginning and thereafter to an increasing degree he faced the others as more or less independent entities and communicated with them as such, addressing and being addressed by them in that manner. This creation of a "social" world out of persons at once mutually dependent and independent differed in kind from all similar undertakings on the part of animals, just as the technical work of man differed in kind from all the animals' works. Apes, too, make use of some stick they happen to have found, as a lever, a digging-tool or a weapon; but that is an affair of chance only: they cannot conceive and produce a tool as an object constituted so and not otherwise and having an existence of its own. And again, many of the insects live in societies built up on a strict division of labour; but it is just this division of labour that governs absolutely their relations with one another; they are all as it were tools; only, their own society is the thing that makes use of them for its "instinctive" purposes; there is no improvisation, no degree, however modest, of mutual independence, no possibility of "free" regard for one another, and thus no person-to-person relationship. Just as the specific technical creations of man mean the conferring of independence on things, so his specific social creation means the conferring of independence on beings of his own kind. It is in the light of this specifically human idiosyncrasy that we have to interpret man's journey with all its ups and downs, and so also the point we have reached on this journey, our great and particular crisis.

In the evolution of mankind hitherto this, then, is the line that predominates: the forming and re-forming of communities on the basis of growing personal independence, their mutual recognition and collaboration on that basis. The two most important steps that the man of early times took on the road to human society can be established with some certainty. The first is that inside the individual clan each individual, through an extremely primitive form of division of labour, was recognized and utilized in his special capacity, so that the clan increasingly took on the character of an ever-renewed association of persons each the vehicle of a different function. The second is that different clans would, under certain conditions, band together in quest of food and for campaigns, and consolidated their mutual help as customs and laws that took firmer and firmer root; so that as once between individuals, so now between communities people discerned and acknowledged differences of nature and function. Wherever genuine human society has since developed it has always been on this same basis of functional autonomy, mutual recognition and mutual responsibility, whether individual or collective. Power-centres of various kinds have split off, organizing and guaranteeing the common order and security of all; but to the political sphere in the stricter sense, the State with its police-system and its bureaucracy, there was always opposed the organic, functionally organized society as such, a great society built up of various societies, the great society in which men lived and worked, competed with one another and helped one another; and in each of the big and little societies composing it, in each of these communes and communities the individual human being, despite all the difficulties and conflicts, felt himself at home as once in the clan, felt himself approved and affirmed in his functional independence and responsibility.

All this changed more and more as the centralistic political principle subordinated the de-centralistic social principle. The crucial thing here was not that the State, particularly in its more or less totalitarian forms, weakened and gradually displaced the free associations, but that the political principle with all its centralistic features percolated into the associations themselves, modifying their structure and their whole inner life, and thus politicized society to an ever-increasing extent. Society's assimilation in the State was accelerated by the fact that, as a result of modern industrial development and its ordered chaos involving the struggle of all against all for access to raw materials and for a larger share of the world-market, there grew up, in place of the old struggles between States, struggles between whole societies. The individual society, feeling itself threatened not only by its neighbours' lust for aggression but also by things in general, knew no way of salvation save in complete submission to the principle of centralized power; and, in the democratic forms of society no less than in its totalitarian forms, it made this its guiding principle. Everywhere the only thing of importance was the minute organization of power, the unquestioning observance of slogans, the saturation of the whole of society with the real or supposed interests of the State. Concurrently with this there is an internal development. In the monstrous confusion of modern life, only thinly disguised by the reliable functioning of the economic and State-apparatus, the individual clings desperately to the collectivity. The little society in which he was embedded cannot help him; only the great collectivities, so he thinks, can do that, and he is all too willing to let himself be deprived of personal responsibility: he only wants to obey. And the most valuable of all goods—the life between man and man—gets lost in the process; the autonomous relationships become meaningless, personal relationships wither; and the very spirit of man hires itself out as a functionary. The personal human being ceases to be the living member of a social body and becomes a cog in the "collective" machine. Just as his degenerate technology is causing man to lose the feel of good work and proportion, so the degrading social life he leads is causing him to lose the feel of community—just when he is so full of the illusion of living in perfect devotion to his community.

A crisis of this kind cannot be overcome by struggling back to an earlier stage of the journey, but only by trying to master the problems as they are, without minimizing them. There is no going back for us, we have to go through with it. But we shall only get through if we know *where* we want to go.

We must begin, obviously, with the establishment of a vital peace which will deprive the political principle of its supremacy over the social principle. And this primary objective cannot in its turn be reached by any devices of political organization, but only by the resolute will of all peoples to cultivate the territories and raw materials of our planet and govern its inhabitants, *together*. At this point, however, we are threatened by a danger greater than all the previous ones: the danger of a gigantic centralization of power covering the whole planet and devouring all free community. Everything depends on not handing the work of planetary management over to the political principle.

Common management is only possible as socialistic management. But if the fatal question for contemporary man is: Can he or can he not decide in favour of, and educate himself up to, a common socialistic economy? then the propriety of the question lies in an inquiry into Socialism itself: what sort of Socialism is it to be, under whose ægis the common economy of man is to come about, if at all?

The ambiguity of the terms we are employing is greater here than anywhere else. People say, for instance, that Socialism is the passing of the control of the means of production out of the hands of the entrepreneurs into the hands of the collectivity; but again, it all depends on what you mean by "collectivity". If it is what we generally call the "State", that is to say, an institution in which a virtually unorganized mass allows its affairs to be conducted by "representation", as they call it, then the chief change in a socialistic society will be this: that the workers will feel themselves represented by the holders of power. But what is representation? Does not the worst defect of modern society lie precisely in everybody letting himself be represented *ad libitum*? And in a "socialistic" society will there not, on top of this passive political representation, be added a passive economic representation, so that, with everybody letting himself be represented by everybody else, we reach a state of practically unlimited representation and hence, ultimately, the reign of practically unlimited centralist accumulation of power? But the more a human group lets itself be represented in the management of its common affairs, and the more it lets itself be represented from outside, the less communal life there is in it and the more impoverished it becomes as a community. For community—not the primitive sort, but the sort possible and appropriate to modern man—declares itself primarily in the common and active management of what it has in common, and without this it cannot exist.

The primary aspiration of all history is a genuine community of human beings—genuine because it is *community all through*. A community that failed to base itself on the actual and communal life of big and little groups living and working together, and on their mutual relationships, would be fictitious and counterfeit. Hence everything depends on whether the collectivity into whose hands the control of the means of pro-

duction passes will facilitate and promote in its very structure
and in all its institutions the genuine common life of the various
groups composing it—on whether, in fact, these groups themselves become proper foci of the productive process; therefore
on whether the masses are so organized in their separate
organizations (the various "communities") as to be as powerful
as the common economy of man permits; therefore on whether
centralist representation only goes as far as the new order of
things absolutely demands. The fatal question does not take
the form of a fundamental Either-Or: it is only a question of
the right line of demarcation that has to be drawn ever anew—
the thousandfold system of demarcation between the spheres
which must of necessity be centralized and those which can
operate in freedom; between the degree of government and the
degree of autonomy; between the law of unity and the claims
of community. The unwearying scrutiny of conditions in terms
of the claims of community, as something continually exposed
to the depredations of centralist power—the *custody of the true*
boundaries, ever changing in accordance with changing historical
circumstances: such would be the task of humanity's spiritual
conscience, a Supreme Court unexampled in kind, the right
true representation of a living idea. A new incarnation is
waiting here for Plato's "custodians".

Representation of an idea, I say: not of a rigid principle but
of a living form that wants to be shaped in the daily stuff of
this earth. Community should not be made into a principle;
it, too, should always satisfy a situation rather than an abstraction. The realization of community, like the realization of any
idea, cannot occur once and for all time: always it must be the
moment's answer to the moment's question, and nothing
more.

In the interests of its vital meaning, therefore, the idea of
community must be guarded against all contamination by
sentimentality or emotionalism. Community is never a mere
attitude of mind, and if it is *feeling* it is an inner disposition
that is felt. Community is the inner disposition or constitution
of a life in common, which knows and embraces in itself hard
"calculation", adverse "chance", the sudden access of
"anxiety". It is community of tribulation and only because of
that community of spirit; community of toil and only because
of that community of salvation. Even those communities which
call the spirit their master and salvation their Promised Land,

the "religious" communities, are community only if they serve their lord and master in the midst of simple, unexalted, unselected reality, a reality not so much chosen by them as sent to them just as it is; they are community only if they prepare the way to the Promised Land through the thickets of this pathless hour. True, it is not "works" that count, but the work of faith does. A community of faith truly exists only when it is a community of work.

The real essence of community is to be found in the fact—manifest or otherwise—that is has a centre. The real beginning of a community is when its members have a common relation to the centre overriding all other relations: the circle is described by the radii, not by the points along its circumference. And the originality of the centre cannot be discerned unless it is discerned as being transpicuous to the light of something divine. All this is true; but the more earthly, the more creaturely, the more attached the centre is, the truer and more transpicuous it will be. This is where the "social" element comes in. Not as something separate, but as the all-pervading realm where man stands the test; and it is here that the truth of the centre is proved. The early Christians were not content with the community that existed alongside or even above the world, and they went into the desert so as to have no more community save with God and no more disturbing world. But it was shown them that God does not wish man to be alone with him; and above the holy impotence of the hermit there rose the Brotherhood. Finally, going beyond St. Benedict, St. Francis entered into alliance with all creatures.

Yet a community need not be "founded". Wherever historical destiny had brought a group of men together in a common fold, there was room for the growth of a genuine community; and there was no need of an altar to the city deity in the midst when the citizens knew they were united round—and by—the Nameless. A living togetherness, constantly renewing itself, was already there, and all that needed strengthening was the immediacy of relationships. In the happiest instances common affairs were deliberated and decided not through representatives but in gatherings in the market-place; and the unity that was felt in public permeated all personal contacts. The danger of seclusion might hang over the community, but the communal spirit banished it; for here this spirit flourished as nowhere else and broke windows for itself in the narrow walls, with a large view of people, mankind and the world.

All this, I may be told, has gone irrevocably and for ever. The modern city has no agora and the modern man has no time for negotiations of which his elected representatives can very well relieve him. The pressure of numbers and the forms of organization have destroyed any real togetherness. Work forges other personal links than does leisure, sport again others than politics, the day is cleanly divided and the soul too. These links are material ones; though we follow our common interests and tendencies together, we have no use for "immediacy". The collectivity is not a warm, friendly gathering but a great link-up of economic and political forces inimical to the play of romantic fancies, only understandable in terms of quantity, expressing itself in actions and effects—a thing which the individual has to belong to with no intimacies of any kind but all the time conscious of his energetic contribution. Any "unions" that resist the inevitable trend of events must disappear. There is still the family, of course, which, as a domestic community, seems to demand and guarantee a modicum of communal life; but it too will either emerge from the crisis in which it is involved, as an association for a common purpose, or else it will perish.

Faced with this medley of correct premises and absurd conclusions I declare in favour of a rebirth of the commune. A rebirth—not a bringing back. It cannot in fact be brought back, although I sometimes think that every touch of helpful neighbourliness in the apartment-house, every wave of warmer comradeship in the lulls and "knock-offs" that occur even in the most perfectly "rationalized" factory, means an addition to the world's community-content; and although a rightly constituted village commune sometimes strikes me as being a more real thing than a parliament; but it cannot be brought back. Yet whether a rebirth of the commune will ensue from the "water and spirit" of the social transformation that is imminent —on this, it seems to me, hangs the whole fate of the human race. An organic commonwealth—and only such commonwealths can join together to form a shapely and articulated race of men—will never build itself up out of individuals but only out of small and ever smaller communities: a nation is a community to the degree that it is a community of communities. If the family does not emerge from the crisis which to-day has all the appearance of a disintegration, purified and renewed, then the State will be nothing more than a machine stoked with the bodies of generations of men. The community that would be capable of such a renewal exists only as a residue. If I speak of its rebirth I am not thinking of a permanent world-situation but an altered one. By the new communes—they might equally well be called the new Co-operatives—I mean the subjects of a changed economy: the collectives into whose hands the control of the means of production is to pass. Once again, everything depends on whether they will be ready.

Just how much economic and political autonomy—for they will of necessity be economic and political units at once—will have to be conceded to them is a technical question that must be asked and answered over and over again; but asked and answered beyond the technical level, in the knowledge that the internal authority of a community hangs together with its external authority. The relationship between centralism and decentralization is a problem which, as we have seen, cannot be approached in principle, but, like everything to do with the relationship between idea and reality, only with great spiritual tact, with the constant and tireless weighing and measuring of the right proportion between them. Centralization—but only so much as is indispensable in the given conditions of time and place. And if the authorities responsible for the drawing and re-drawing of lines of demarcation keep an alert conscience, the relations between the base and the apex of the power-pyramid will be very different from what they are now, even in States that call themselves Communist, i.e. struggling for community. There will have to be a system of representation, too, in the sort of social pattern I have in mind; but it will not, as now, be composed of the pseudo-representatives of amorphous masses of electors but of representatives well tested in the life and work of the communes. The represented will not, as they are to-day, be bound to their representatives by some windy abstraction, by the mere phraseology of a party-programme, but concretely, through common action and common experience.

The essential thing, however, is that the process of community-building shall run all through the relations of the communes with one another. Only a community of communities merits the title of Commonwealth.

The picture I have hastily sketched will doubtless be laid among the documents of "Utopian Socialism" until the storm turns them up again. Just as I do not believe in Marx's "gestation" of the new form, so I do not believe either in Bakunin's virgin-birth from the womb of Revolution. But I do believe in the meeting of idea and fate in the creative hour.

EPILOGUE

AN EXPERIMENT
THAT DID NOT FAIL

THE era of advanced Capitalism has broken down the structure of society. The society which preceded it was composed of different societies; it was complex, and pluralistic in structure. This is what gave it its peculiar social vitality and enabled it to resist the totalitarian tendencies inherent in the pre-revolutionary centralistic State, though many elements were very much weakened in their autonomous life. This resistance was broken by the policy of the French Revolution, which was directed against the special rights of all free associations. Thereafter centralism in its new, capitalistic form succeeded where the old had failed: in atomizing society. Exercising control over the machines and, with their help, over the whole society, Capitalism wants to deal only with individuals; and the modern State aids and abets it by progressively dispossessing groups of their autonomy. The militant organizations which the proletariat erected against Capitalism—Trades Unions in the economic sphere and the Party in the political—are unable in the nature of things to counteract this process of dissolution, since they have no access to the life of society itself and its foundations: production and consumption. Even the transfer of capital to the State is powerless to modify the social structure, even when the State establishes a network of compulsory associations, which, having no autonomous life, are unfitted to become the cells of a new socialist society.

From this point of view the heart and soul of the Co-operative Movement is to be found in the trend of a society towards structural renewal, the re-acquisition, in new tectonic forms, of the internal social relationships, the establishment of a new *consociatio consociationum*. It is (as I have shown) a fundamental error to view this trend as romantic or utopian merely because in its early stages it had romantic reminiscences and utopian fantasies. At bottom it is thoroughly topical and constructive; that is to say, it aims at changes which, in the given circumstances and with the means at its disposal, are feasible. And, psychologically speaking, it is based on one of the eternal human needs, even though this need has often been forcibly suppressed or rendered insensible: the need of man to feel his own house as a room in some greater, all-embracing structure in which he is at home, to feel that the other inhabitants of it with whom he lives and works are all acknowledging and confirming his individual existence. An association based on community of views and aspirations alone cannot satisfy this need; the only thing that can do that is an association which makes for communal living. But here the co-operative organization of production or consumption proves, each in its own way, inadequate, because both touch the individual only at a certain point and do not mould his actual life. On account of their merely partial or functional character all such organizations are equally unfitted to act as cells of a new society. Both these partial forms have undergone vigorous development, but the Consumer Co-operatives only in highly bureaucratic forms and the Producer Co-operatives in highly specialized forms: they are less able to embrace the whole life of society to-day than ever. The consciousness of this fact is leading to the synthetic form: the Full Co-operative. By far the most powerful effort in this direction is the Village Commune, where communal living is based on the amalgamation of production and consumption, production being understood not exclusively as agriculture alone but as the organic union of agriculture with industry and with the handicrafts as well.

The repeated attempts that have been made during the last 150 years, both in Europe and America, to found village settlements of this kind, whether communistic or co-operative in the narrower sense, have mostly met with failure.[1] I would apply the word "failure" not merely to those settlements, or attempts at settlements, which after a more or less short-lived existence either disintegrated completely or took on a Capitalist complexion, thus going over to the enemy camp; I would also

[1] Of course, I am not dealing here with the otherwise successful "socio-economic organizations, used by governmental or semi-governmental agencies to improve rural conditions" (Infield, *Co-operative Communities at Work*, p. 63).

apply it to those that maintained themselves in isolation. For the real, the truly structural task of the new Village Communes begins with their *federation*, that is, their union under the same principle that operates in their internal structure. Hardly anywhere has it come to this. Even where, as with the Dukhobors in Canada, a sort of federative union exists, the federation itself continues to be isolated and exerts no attractive and educative influence on society as a whole, with the result that the task never gets beyond its beginnings and, consequently, there can be no talk of success in the socialist sense. It is remarkable that Kropotkin saw in these two elements—isolation of the settlements from one another and isolation from the rest of society—the efficient causes of their failure even as ordinarily understood.

The socialistic task can only be accomplished to the degree that the new Village Commune, combining the various forms of production and uniting production and consumption, exerts a structural influence on the amorphous urban society. The influence will only make itself felt to the full if, and to the extent that, further technological developments facilitate and actually require the decentralization of industry; but even now a pervasive force is latent in the modern communal village, and it may spread to the towns. It must be emphasized again that the tendency we are dealing with is constructive and topical: it would be romantic and utopian to want to destroy the towns, as once it was romantic and utopian to want to destroy the machines, but it is constructive and topical to try to transform the town organically in the closest possible alliance with technological developments and to turn it into an aggregate composed of smaller units. Indeed, many countries to-day show significant beginnings in this respect.

As I see history and the present, there is only one all-out effort to create a Full Co-operative which justifies our speaking of success in the socialistic sense, and that is the Jewish Village Commune in its various forms, as found in Palestine. No doubt it, too, is up against grave problems in the sphere of internal relationships, federation, and influence on society at large, but it alone has proved its vitality in all three spheres. Nowhere else in the history of communal settlements is there this tireless groping for the form of community-life best suited to this particular human group, nowhere else this continual trying and trying again, this going to it and getting down to it, this critical awareness, this sprouting of new branches from the same stem and out of the same formative impulse. And nowhere else is there this alertness to one's own problems, this constant facing up to them, this tough will to come to terms with them, and this indefatigable struggle—albeit seldom expressed in words—to overcome them. Here, and here alone, do we find in the emergent community organs of self-knowledge whose very sensitiveness has constantly reduced its members to despair—but this is a despair that destroys wishful thinking only to raise up in its stead a greater hope which is no longer emotionalism but sheer work. Thus on the soberest survey and on the soberest reflection one can say that, in this one spot in a world of partial failures, we can recognize a non-failure—and, such as it is, a signal non-failure.

What are the reasons for this? We could not get to know the peculiar character of this co-operative colonization better than by following up these reasons.

One element in these reasons has been repeatedly pointed out: that the Jewish Village Commune in Palestine owes its existence not to a doctrine but to a situation, to the needs, the stress, the demands of the situation. In establishing the "Kvuza" or Village Commune the primary thing was not ideology but work. This is certainly correct, but with one limitation. True, the point was to solve certain problems of work and construction which the Palestinian reality forced on the settlers, by collaborating; what a loose conglomeration of individuals could not, in the nature of things, hope to overcome, or even try to overcome, things being what they were, the collective could try to do and actually succeeded in doing. But what is called the "ideology"—I personally prefer the old but untarnished word "Ideal"—was not just something to be added afterwards, that would justify the accomplished facts. In the spirit of the members of the first Palestinian Communes ideal motives joined hands with the dictates of the hour; and in the motives there was a curious mixture of memories of the Russian *Artel*, impressions left over from reading the so-called "utopian" Socialists, and the half-unconscious after-effects of the Bible's teachings about social justice. The important thing is that this ideal motive remained loose and pliable in almost every respect. There were various dreams about the future: people saw before them a new, more comprehensive form of the family, they saw themselves as the advance guard of the

Workers' Movement, as the direct instrument for the realization of Socialism, as the prototype of the new society; they had as their goal the creation of a new man and a new world. But nothing of this ever hardened into a cut-and-dried programme. These men did not, as everywhere else in the history of co-operative settlements, bring a plan with them, a plan which the concrete situation could only fill out, not modify; the ideal gave an impetus but no dogma, it stimulated but did not dictate.

More important, however, is that, behind the Palestinian situation that set the tasks of work and reconstruction, there was the historical situation of a people visited by a great external crisis and responding to it with a great inner change. Further, this historical situation threw up an élite—the "Chaluzim" or pioneers—drawn from all classes of the people and thus beyond class. The form of life that befitted this élite was the Village Commune, by which I mean not a single note but the whole scale, ranging from the social structure of "mutual aid" to the Commune itself. This form was the best fitted to fulfil the tasks of the central Chaluzim, and at the same time the one in which the social ideal could materially influence the national idea. As the historical conditions have shown, it was impossible for this élite and the form of life it favoured, to become static or isolated; all its tasks, everything it did, its whole pioneering spirit made it the centre of attraction and a central influence. The Pioneer spirit ("Chaluziuth") is, in every part of it, related to the growth of a new and transformed national community; the moment it grew self-sufficient it would have lost its soul. The Village Commune, as the nucleus of the evolving society, had to exert a powerful pull on the people dedicated to this evolution, and it had not merely to educate its friends and associates for genuine communal living, but also to exercise a formative structural effect on the social periphery. The dynamics of history determined the dynamic character of the relations between Village Commune and society.

This character suffered a considerable setback when the tempo of the crisis in the outer world became so rapid, and its symptoms so drastic, that the inner change could not keep pace with them. To the extent that Palestine had been turned from the one and only land of the "Aliyah"—ascent—into a country of immigrants, a quasi-Chaluziuth came into being alongside the genuine Chaluziuth. The pull exerted by the Commune did not abate, but its educative powers were not adapted to the influx of very different human material, and this material sometimes succeeded in influencing the tone of the community. At the same time the Commune's relations with society at large underwent a change. As the structure of the latter altered, it withdrew more and more from the transforming influence of the focal cells, indeed, it began in its turn to exert an influence on them—not always noticeable at first, but unmistakable to-day—by seizing on certain essential elements in them and assimilating them to itself.

In the life of peoples, and particularly peoples who find themselves in the midst of some historical crisis, it is of crucial importance whether genuine élites (which means élites that do not usurp but are called to their central function) arise, whether these élites remain loyal to their duty to society, establishing a relationship to it rather than to themselves, and finally, whether they have the power to replenish and renew themselves in a manner conformable with their task. The historical destiny of the Jewish settlements in Palestine brought the élite of the Chaluzim to birth, and it found its social nuclear form in the Village Commune. Another wave of this same destiny has washed up, together with the quasi-Chaluzim, a problem for the real Chaluzim élite. It has caused a problem that was always latent to come to the surface. They have not yet succeeded in mastering it and yet must master it before they can reach the next stage of their task. The inner tension between those who take the *whole* responsibility for the community on their shoulders and those who somehow evade it, can be resolved only at a very deep level.

The point where the problem emerges is neither the individual's relationship to the idea nor his relationship to the community nor yet to work; on all these points even the quasi-Chaluzim gird up their loins and do by and large what is expected of them. The point where the problem emerges, where people are apt to slip, is in their relationship to their fellows. By this I do not mean the question, much discussed in its day, of the intimacy that exists in the small and the loss of this intimacy in the big Kvuza; I mean something that has nothing whatever to do with the size of the Commune. It is not a matter of intimacy at all; this appears when it must, and if it is lacking, that's all there is to it. The question is rather one of openness. A real community need not consist of people who are perpetually together; but it must consist of people who, precisely because they are comrades, have mutual access to one another and are ready for one another. A real community is one which in every point of its being possesses, potentially at least, the whole character of community. The internal questions of a community are thus in reality questions relating to its own genuineness, hence to its inner strength and stability. The men who created the Jewish Communes in Palestine instinctively knew this; but the instinct no longer seems to be as common and alert as it was. Yet it is in this most important field that we find that remorselessly clear-sighted collective self-observation and self-criticism to which I have already drawn attention. But to understand and value it aright we must see it together with the amazingly positive relationship—amounting to a regular faith—which these men have to the inmost being of their Commune. The two things are two sides of the same spiritual world and neither can be understood without the other.

In order to make the causes of the non-failure of these Jewish communal settlements sufficiently vivid, in Palestine, I began with the non-doctrinaire character of their origins. This character also determined their development in all essentials. New forms and new intermediate forms were constantly branching off—in complete freedom. Each one grew out of the particular social and spiritual needs as these came to light—in complete freedom, and each one acquired, even in the initial stages, its own ideology—in complete freedom, each struggling to propagate itself and spread and establish its proper sphere—all in complete freedom. The champions of the various forms each had his say, the pros and cons of each individual form were frankly and fiercely debated—always, however, on the plane which everybody accepted as obvious: the common cause and common task, where each form recognized the relative justice of all the other forms in their special functions. All this is unique in the history of co-operative settlements. What is more: nowhere, as far as I see, in the history of the Socialist movement were men so deeply involved in the process of differentiation and yet so intent on preserving the principle of integration.

The various forms and intermediate forms that arose in this

way at different times and in different situations represented different kinds of social structure. The people who built them were generally aware of this as also of the particular social and spiritual needs that actuated them. They were not aware to the same extent that the different forms corresponded to different human types and that just as new forms branched off from the original Kvuza, so new types branched off from the original Chaluz type, each with its special mode of being and each demanding its particular sort of realization. More often than not it was economic and suchlike external factors that led certain people to break away from one form and attach themselves to another. But in the main it happened that each type looked for the social realization of its peculiarities in this particular form and, on the whole, found it there. And not only was each form based on a definite type, it moulded and keeps on moulding this type. It was and is intent on developing it; the constitution, organization and educational system of each form are—no matter how consciously or unconsciously— dedicated to this end. Thus something has been produced which is essentially different from all the social experiments that have ever been made: not a laboratory where everybody works for himself, alone with his problems and plans, but an experimental station where, on common soil, different colonies or "cultures" are tested out according to different methods for a common purpose.

Yet here, too, a problem emerged, no longer within the individual group but in the relation of the groups to one another; nor did it come from without, it came from within— in fact, from the very heart of the principle of freedom.

Even in its first undifferentiated form a tendency towards federation was innate in the Kvuza, to merge the Kvuzoth in some higher social unit; and a very important tendency it was, since it showed that the Kvuza implicitly understood that it was the cell of a newly structured society. With the splitting off and proliferation of the various forms, from the semi-individualistic form which jealously guarded personal independence in its domestic economy, way of life, children's education, etc., to the pure Communistic form, the single unit was supplanted by a series of units in each of which a definite form of colony and a more or less definite human type con- stituted itself on a federal basis. The fundamental assumption was that the local groups would combine on the same principle of solidarity and mutual help as reigned within the individual group. But the trend towards a larger unit is far from having atrophied in the process. On the contrary, at least in the Kibbuz or Collectivist Movement, it asserts itself with great force and clarity; it recognizes the federative Kibbuzim—units where the local groups have pooled their various aspirations— as a provisional structure; indeed, a thoughtful leader of their movement calls them a substitute for a Commune of Communes. Apart from the fact, however, that individual forms, especially, for instance, the "Moshavim" or semi-individualistic Labour Settlements—though these do not fall short of any of the other forms in the matter of communal economic control and mutual help—are already too far removed from the basic form to be included in a unitary plan, in the Kibbuz Movement itself subsidiary organizations stand in the way of the trend towards unification which wants to embrace and absorb them. Each has developed its own special character and consolidated it in the unit, and it is natural that each should incline to view unification as an extension of its own influence. But something else has been added that has led to an enormous intensification of this attitude on the part of the single units: political development. Twenty years ago a leader of one of the big units could say emphatically: "We are a community and not a Party." This has radically changed in the meantime, and the conditions for unification have been aggravated accordingly. The lamentable fact has emerged that the all-important attitude of neighbourly relationship has not been adequately developed, although not a few cases are on record of a flourishing and rich village giving generous help to a young and poor neighbour which belonged to another unit. In these circumstances the great struggle that has broken out on the question of unification, particularly in the last decade, is the more remarkable. Nobody who is a Socialist at heart can read the great document of this struggle, the Hebrew compilation entitled *The Kibbuz and the Kvuza*, edited by the late labour leader Berl Kaznelson, without being lost in admiration of the high-minded passion with which these two camps battled with one another for genuine unity. The union will probably not be attained save as the outcome of a situation that makes it absolutely necessary. But that the men of the Jewish Communes have laboured so strenuously with one another and against one another for the emergence of a *communitas communi-*

tatum, that is to say, for a structurally new society—this will
not be forgotten in the history of mankind's struggle for self-
renewal.

I have said that I see in this bold Jewish undertaking a
"signal non-failure". I cannot say: a signal success. To
become that, much has still to be done. Yet it is in this way,
in this kind of tempo, with such setbacks, disappointments, and
new ventures, that the real changes are accomplished in this
our mortal world.

But can one speak of this non-failure as "signal"? I have
pointed out the peculiar nature of the premises and conditions
that led to it. And what one of its own representatives has
said of the Kvuza, that it is a typically Palestinian product,
is true of all these forms.

Still, if an experiment conducted under certain conditions
has proved successful up to a point, we can set about varying
it under other, less favourable, conditions.

There can hardly be any doubt that we must regard the last
war as the end of the prelude to a world crisis. This crisis will
probably break out—after a sombre "interlude" that cannot
last very long—first among some of the nations of the West, who
will be able to restore their shattered economy in appearance
only. They will see themselves faced with the immediate need
for radical socialization, above all the expropriation of the land.
It will then be of absolutely decisive importance *who* is the real
subject of an economy so transformed, and who is the owner of
the social means of production. Is it to be the central authority
in a highly centralized State, or the social units of urban and
rural workers, living and producing on a communal basis, and
their representative bodies? In the latter case the remodelled
organs of the State will discharge the functions of adjustment
and administration only. On these issues will largely depend
the growth of a new society and a new civilization. The essential
point is to decide on the fundamentals: a re-structuring of
society as a League of Leagues, and a reduction of the State
to its proper function, which is to maintain unity; or a devouring
of an amorphous society by the omnipotent State; Socialist
Pluralism or so-called Socialist Unitarianism. The right proportion, tested anew every day according to changing conditions, between group-freedom and collective order; or
absolute order imposed indefinitely for the sake of an era of
freedom alleged to follow "of its own accord". So long as

Russia has not undergone an essential inner change—and to-day we have no means of knowing when and how that will come to pass—we must designate one of the two poles of Socialism between which our choice lies, by the formidable name of "Moscow". The other, I would make bold to call "Jerusalem".

INDEX